Better Homes and Gardens®

new teen book

by Wade F. Horn, Ph.D., and Carol Keough

Meredith® Books
Des Moines, Iowa

Better Homes and Gardens® Books
An imprint of Meredith® Books

New Teen Book
Associate Design Director: Ken Carlson
Copy Chief: Catherine Hamrick
Copy and Production Editor: Terri Fredrickson
Contributing Copy Editor: Ed Malles
Contributing Proofreaders: Neala M. Ellingson, Cynthia M. Johnson, Debra Morris Smith
Contributing Photographer: Chip Simons
Indexer: Sharon Duffy
Electronic Production Coordinator: Paula Forest
Editorial and Design Assistants: Kaye Chabot, Mary Lee Gavin, Karen Schirm
Production Director: Douglas M. Johnston
Production Manager: Pam Kvitne
Assistant Prepress Manager: Marjorie J. Schenkelberg

Meredith® Books
Editor in Chief: James D. Blume
Design Director: Matt Strelecki
Managing Editor: Gregory H. Kayko
Executive Health Editor: Alice Feinstein

Director, Sales & Marketing, Retail: Michael A. Peterson
Director, Sales & Marketing, Special Markets: Rita McMullen
Director, Sales & Marketing, Home & Garden Center Channel: Ray Wolf
Director, Operations: George A. Susral

Vice President, General Manager: Jamie L. Martin

Better Homes and Gardens® **Magazine**
Editor in Chief: Jean LemMon

Meredith Publishing Group
President, Publishing Group: Christopher M. Little
Vice President, Consumer Marketing & Development: Hal Oringer

Meredith Corporation
Chairman and Chief Executive Officer: William T. Kerr

Chairman of the Executive Committee: E. T. Meredith III

NOTICE TO READERS: This book is intended to provide you with information about parenting a teenager. It is not intended to be a medical guide or to serve as a substitute for advice from your doctor. Every teenager's needs are unique. Diagnosis and treatment must be done through health care professionals.

Write to us at: Better Homes and Gardens® Books, Health Editorial Department, 1716 Locust St., Des Moines, IA 50309-3023.
If you would like to purchase additional copies of any of our books, check wherever quality books are sold.

"Adolescence is a new birth, for the higher and more completely human traits are now born ... Important functions previously nonexistent arise ... It is the age of sentiment and of religion, of rapid fluctuation of mood ... Self-feeling and ambition are increased, and every trait and faculty is liable to exaggeration and excess. It is all a marvelous new birth."

—G. Stanley Hall, *who pioneered the study of adolescence in developmental psychology*

"It is a popular notion that adolescents career out of control, are hypnotized by peer pressure or manipulated by demons for six years or so, and then if they don't get messed up or hurt or killed, they become sensible adults. That's ridiculous. The youngsters I have spoken to are trying the best they can in the present world to do what is right for them."

—Patricia Hersch, *author of* A Tribe Apart

Dedications

For my wife, Claudia, who sustains me with her love, and my two teenage daughters, Christen and Caroline, who keep me honest and fill me with joy. —Wade Horn

My work in this book is dedicated to my dear husband Bill (my coconspirator in raising teenagers) as well as to Bradley, Jeffrey, Fiona, Josiah, and Samantha.—Carol Keough

table of contents

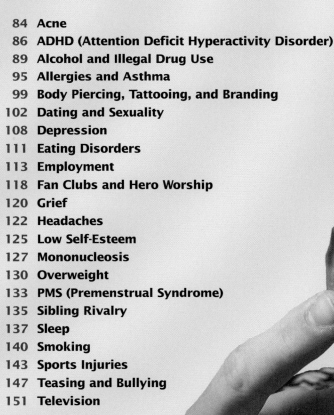

introduction

teens
happen

Ladies and Gentlemen, the captain has turned on the fasten seat belt sign. There are some bumpy years ahead.

When you made that fateful decision some 12 or so years ago to have a child, deep down inside you knew that sooner or later this day would come. Now it has. And you're going to have to learn to live with this … teenager.

You've undoubtedly been asking yourself, "How could the cutest, most adorable, cuddly and adoring child that ever graced this planet turn into a phone-hogging, mood-swinging, parent-defying, fast-food gulping, boy-crazy (or girl-crazy), know-it-all? What did we do wrong?"

Of course, you didn't do anything wrong. Teenagers just are. The fact is adolescence is as necessary a stage in a child's development as any other. Without it, our children couldn't become what we ultimately want them to become: adults. That, in a nutshell, is your job—helping your teenager become an adult. It isn't an easy task. But given a certain amount of knowledge and skill it is an eminently doable task.

First, a little perspective. As difficult as it can be at times to live with a teenager, being one is even harder. We know. We parents were teenagers once ourselves. It'll be helpful to keep this in mind as you set your sights on parenting this new and seemingly unfamiliar creature.

But just in case you've completely repressed all memories of your own teenage experience (and who hasn't repressed at least a few of them?), here's a brief reminder. After a period of relative quiescence, children emerge on the other side of elementary school experiencing many rapid changes, including the biological (Oops! There's another pimple!), cognitive (What kind of moral and religious beliefs should I adhere to?), emotional (Whoa! Am I in love? YES! ... At least I think I am.), and psychosocial (Should I listen to my friends or my parents?). Negotiating all of these changes all at once isn't easy. You'd be moody, too.

But there is good news, and here it is. Believe it or not, you—your teenager's know-nothing parents—are still the most important influence in your child's life.

Teenagers are like clams. They open up just for a moment in order to take in a little nourishment or expel some dirt. But then they clam up tight again. If you're around when they open up, you have a chance to see something truly beautiful inside.

Nothing, not their friends, not their teachers, not even rock music (yikes!), has as much influence on what your teen does, thinks, and believes as you do. Survey after survey shows that teens continue, despite their protestations, to look to their parents for direction and help in making sense of their expanding universe. What's more, most teens actually like their parents. Huh? That's right. While the teenage years may have their share of arguments and conflict, most teenagers report having a good relationship with their parents. And those that don't, wish they did.

Another piece of good news is that most parent-teen conflict is over little things. Although most parents of new teens are most fearful of conflicts around sex, drugs, and alcohol, the most frequent conflicts usually involve such things as keeping a clean room, clothing choices, homework, and hairstyles. When it comes to the big stuff, most teens respect and behave according to their parents' values—so long, that is, as their parents effectively communicate what their values are on the things that really count. (We'll talk more about this later.)

Research shows, moreover, that when parent-teen conflict occurs within the context of an overall supportive relationship, it actually can result in all sorts of positive experiences, such as changing behavior constructively, encouraging more realistic perspective, helping to develop a sense of self separate from the family, and teaching negotiation and conflict-resolution skills. Unfortunately, the same research shows that when parent-teen conflict occurs outside of an overall supportive relationship, it can have dire consequences, including depression, drug and alcohol abuse, running away from home, and teen pregnancy.

So while some parent-teenager conflict may be inevitable, big problems aren't.

The key to success is the quality of the overall relationship you have with your teen. Those parents who maintain good communication with their teenagers and effectively set age-appropriate limits will end up rearing kids who not only survive adolescence, but emerge on the other side of their teen years as competent, caring, and responsible adults.

How to Use This Book

This book is organized into two major sections. The first section is designed to be read from start to finish. It provides an overview of the biological and psychosocial changes facing today's teens. It also suggests ways that you, the parent, can best help your adolescent through this difficult period with good communication and effective limit setting. This section concludes with a discussion of ways to teenage-proof your marriage—or, if you're not married, suggestions for parenting teens as a single or stepparent.

The second half of the book is organized around common problems facing teenagers along with good, common-sense solutions. You can either choose to read this half of the book in one sitting, or simply look up the areas about which you are most interested. Although in this section we cover many serious problems that teens and their parents face—such as alcohol and illicit drug use, depression and suicide, eating disorders, and teen pregnancy—this book is not intended as a substitute for professional counseling or therapy. Indeed, our focus is primarily prevention oriented. If your family is experiencing significant health or emotional problems, we strongly recommend you seek professional help.

We hope as you read this book, you will keep this one last thing in mind. Adolescence is not all conflict and strife. It also has its share of unique and wonderful joys—like when your teen unexpectedly cuddles up with you on the couch, brags about you to his friends under the impression that you're not listening, or comes downstairs all dressed up in formal wear for the very first time. Paying attention to these moments will help you maintain perspective during your umpteenth argument about why a small little hole filled with a gold hoop in the side of your teen's nose is not such a good idea.

Former U.S. Labor Secretary Robert Reich put it this way:

"[Teenagers] are like clams. They open up just for a moment in order to take in a little nourishment or expel some dirt. But then they clam up tight again. If you're around when they open up, you have a chance to see something truly beautiful inside. Maybe a small stone turning into a gleaming pearl. Maybe shiny smooth inside, still vulnerable. And you have a quick chance to connect.

"But you have to be there in that moment. The clam shuts in an instant, and then you can't see or do a thing..."

So be watchful for the pearl inside your teenager.

It is there—and it is precious indeed.

1

the great change

Puberty. It's an unsettling time for many teens. But let's face it, it's also unsettling for parents.

Parents may be more than a little uneasy with this transitional period in their son's or daughter's life. They're not sure what to expect. How can they tell when their youngster is entering puberty? What should they tell their child about it?

"Puberty is such a nebulous term," says Sloan Beth Karver, M.D., assistant clinical professor of Primary Education and Community Service at Allegheny University in Philadelphia. "It happens over such a long span of time that it's hard for a parent to know exactly when a child enters puberty. Certainly there are hormonal changes even before a parent may see any outward sign."

But outward signs soon do become apparent.

Emerging to Adulthood

Kids entering puberty are growing very fast—so fast they may lose their sense of personal space. As a result, they can be pretty clumsy. They tip over glasses with their elbows, walk into door frames, and literally trip over their own two fast-growing feet.

They may be embarrassed by hair sprouting in unlikely places, and devastated when they break out in pimples. Emotionally, some kids are ready to tackle the world but, at the same time, they're also too shy to pick up the phone and make a date.

Girls, who begin to mature earlier than boys, often feel both self-conscious and proud of their changing bodies. Boys cringe when they speak with a voice that cracks and yodels. But they like growing taller and more muscular.

Kids can feel mighty threatened at times by the process of becoming an adult. (It's scary to leave the comfort and security of childhood!)

Both boys and girls experience emotions that are stronger than those in their pasts. They root passionately for the home team, cry desperately over a friend's perceived snub, and loathe driving Dad's eight-year-old (way uncool) sedan. They may rage against your house rules, a curfew, a refusal to increase their allowance. Not fair, they yell as they slam the door shut.

They turn their rooms into shrines to their favorite music, sports, or film stars. Their devotion to the unreachable Adored One can be sincere, desperate, and deep. And, whatever the emotion your teenager is experiencing, you can be sure that it's set at full volume.

Welcome to your teenager's puberty—the growth spurts, menstruation, ejaculation, pubic hair, body hair, flight toward independence, hero worship, puppy love, and everything else that goes along with it!

So how do you help your teen cope with the astonishing physical and emotional upheaval of puberty? How? You prepare ahead of time.

Some of the more important conversations you will have with your teen are about puberty. Kids can feel mighty threatened at times by the process of becoming an adult. (It's scary to leave the comfort and security of childhood!) Their unease is heightened when they pick up information from their friends about "stuff" that sounds "gross" and "weird."

So that's where you come in, parents.

A Big Time for Small Talk

It's your job to explain puberty to your teenager in a way that makes the change seem quite normal. After all, it is normal! Spelling out the process makes the inevitable physical changes predictable, and therefore more acceptable.

Experts say that it's best to discuss the process before puberty is upon your son or daughter. A good time to talk, they say, is when kids are preadolescent—even before middle school.

These conversations don't have to be a big, formal deal. Instead, look for opportunities that daily living presents. Perhaps you could reflect on a TV commercial that advertises sanitary pads, comment on the birth of a neighbor's baby, or mention the fact that 17-year-old Cousin Kenny is trying to grow a mustache. Talk about your own puberty: your problem with acne, what your mother told you about menstruation, when you learned to shave, your first date.

"Did you know," Mother might venture after seeing that television commercial, "back when I first got my period, sanitary pads didn't have wings? Of course, that was a long time ago. I guess I was thirteen." And so, you're on your way to the kind of casual conversation that allows your daughter to easily ask questions. Or, perhaps, just listen.

Keep your talks short, but let your teen know that you think the information is important. Do not go off into a long "birds-and-bees" lecture that may overwhelm your teenager with too much information at once.

Understand that your son or daughter may need you now more than ever—and be too confused, embarrassed, or shy to broach the subject of puberty. Make a point of telling your teen that he or she can talk to you about anything.

Because your teenager is at an age when it's normal and expected for him or her to begin establishing some independence, it becomes your job to keep a dialogue going on these topics.

Growth Curves These growth curves show the normal range of both height and weight for American boys and girls between the ages of 7 and 18. The shaded areas represent the normal range. The bottom of each pink and blue shaded area represents the 5th percentile, the top of the shaded area represents the 95th percentile.

Plot your teenager's percentile in height by finding his or her age along the bottom of the chart. Next, find your teen's height along the left side of the chart. Draw a line up from your teen's age, and another line across from your teen's height. The point where the two lines meet shows his or her percentile.

If, for example, your 12-year-old son is 60 inches tall, he is in the 75th percentile. That figure shows that he is taller than 74% of all other 12-year-old boys, and shorter than 25% of other 12-year-old boys.

Use the same procedure to plot your teen's weight percentile.

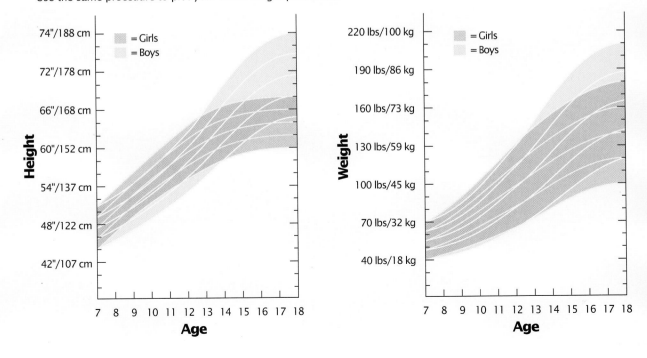

"It's very important for parents to keep the lines of communication open, so that their child can ask for help if it's needed," says Dr. Karver. "And, in today's society, sometimes it's needed desperately.

"The next best thing," she says, "is for a child to have a nice relationship with the family doctor. If a child is not comfortable discussing a situation or problem with parents, he or she can ask the doctor for direction or guidance."

Puberty's Progress

Puberty is defined as a period of rapid physical growth and development that takes place between childhood and adult life. The changes during puberty happen because boys' and girls' bodies are becoming mature enough to reproduce.

These changes in the body are caused by hormones. Some changes are actually the same for boys and girls, but others—obviously—are quite different.

The body-changing process starts in the brain. A part of the brain called the hypothalamus begins to secrete a certain hormone in periodic bursts. The hormone is called luteinizing hormone-releasing hormone (LHRH). This hormone then causes the pituitary gland to release more hormones called gonadotropins. These hormones, in turn, stimulate the ovaries in girls to make estrogen, and the testes in boys to make testosterone. All these hormones together bring about sexual maturation.

Boys Will Be—Men

Sometime between the ages of 12 and 18, your son's body will begin to change into a man's body. Most boys start showing physical changes at about 12 or 13 years of age, but each boy has his own schedule for development. It is considered normal to start as early as 9 or as late as 14 or 15. Usually, a boy's puberty lasts about three years. By age 18, most boys will have grown almost to their adult height, but their muscles still will continue to develop.

Male hormones cause increased muscle mass. You'll see their greatest effect in the sinewy muscles of your son's upper chest and shoulders. Male hormones also lengthen bones, giving men thicker, broader shoulders, as well as longer arms and legs. Usually, the first sign of puberty is the subtle growth of the testicles and scrotum. After a while, the penis starts growing, too. These changes are caused by the male hormone testosterone, which is made in the testicles.

Boys with Breasts

It was a very hot summer day, but Jason absolutely refused to go to the pool. He was adamant. He did not want his friends to see him in swim trunks. Why? Jason appeared to be growing small breasts.

The condition is called gynecomastia, or male breast swelling. And it's very common. In fact, 6 out of 10 teen boys experience it.

In this condition, the area around the nipples appears to bud and feels tender. The change is probably related to the hormone soup of puberty. Levels of male and female hormones increase in both boys and girls, and so it appears that the growth of breast tissue in boys may be a response to the higher levels of female hormones in their bodies.

But sometimes gynecomastia is also an unwanted side effect of a medication such as one used to treat asthma. And sometimes what looks like gynecomastia really is simply obesity.

Usually, the problem goes away by itself in about a year or two. Do call a doctor, however, if your son is on medication when the condition develops, or if it appears before puberty begins. Also make an appointment if your son is like Jason—a boy who needs diagnosis and reassurance.

precocious puberty

Sexual development in little kids (girls age 8 and boys age 10) is considered precocious puberty and can create problems.

About one in every 10,000 children in the United States starts puberty prematurely. While the disorder affects both sexes, it's more common in girls than boys.

Precocious puberty, like normal puberty, brings about the appearance of sexual characteristics. That's because the hormonal changes responsible for early puberty are the same as those that trigger normal puberty.

The main problem with precocious puberty, however, is not sex related. The big problem is one of growth, of achieving a normal height. It's a particularly serious problem for boys.

Children who start puberty prematurely are tall for their age because they have gone through the growth spurt that's triggered by sex hormones. But since their skeleton matures and growth stops at an earlier-than-normal age, they never achieve their full adult height. Boys often grow to be no taller than 5 feet 2 inches, and half of the girls get no taller than 5 feet.

Another problem with precocious puberty is one of social acceptance. Nine-year-old girls with breasts will be teased and taunted. Tall, froggy-voiced boys can easily feel out of place among their shorter friends.

Much of the time precocious puberty just happens. But some cases result from a benign tumor growing on the part of the brain that releases the hormone that triggers puberty. In boys, the disorder may be inherited—passed directly from father to son or indirectly from the maternal grandfather. If your child is showing signs of premature sexual development, it's important to make an appointment with the doctor for evaluation and possible treatment. No matter what the treatment (if any), you have a role to play as a parent.

> **The main problem with precocious puberty is one of growth, of achieving a normal height.**

The way you handle these early changes makes a big difference in the way your child will cope. Social workers at the National Institute of Child Health and Human Development (NICHD) suggest that you clearly explain what is happening to him or her. Tell your child that what is occurring is a normal process, but that it's happening a little too soon. Explain that doctors may be able to stop this early sexual development, and maybe even reverse it.

Treatment is usually aimed at changing the body's hormonal balance. Medications—Supprelin and Synarel—can stop, and even reverse, premature sexual development. There is another experimental therapy, announced by the NICHD, that can interfere with the chain of hormonal events that results in sexual maturation. Menstruation, ovulation, and sperm production stop, and sexual development is reversed in many cases. The best result is that bone development becomes normal, so that kids can grow for a longer time, and grow taller.

At an appropriate age, the treatment is stopped and sexual maturation begins again.

This therapy is considered experimental, and for that reason any long-term effects are unknown. NICHD says there have been no adverse short-term effects. Write to the NICHD, P.O. Box 29111, Washington, DC 20040 for further information.

As the amount of testosterone increases, the scrotum darkens. The penis and testicles start to grow. Often one testicle is larger than the other. The condition is absolutely normal but may concern your son. Be reassuring. There are also

Puberty is defined as a period of rapid physical growth and development that takes place between childhood and adult life.

changes to male organs taking place on the inside the body. (The prostate gland, which provides fluid for the sperm, and seminal vesicles, which transport it, also begin to increase in size.)

At about the same time that the male genitalia are maturing, pubic hair also begins to grow. Underarm and facial hair will come later.

The testicles will start to produce sperm, which are released in a white fluid called semen. Ejaculation isn't possible, however, until the prostate and seminal vesicles are mature.

About a year after the testes have begun to grow, your son may experience his first ejaculation. Often, it happens at night when he is sleeping. It usually occurs unexpectedly. This first ejaculation is the body's way of letting your son know that he is physically able to father children.

At about age 14—but this age is not written in stone—most boys will shoot up in height. And their voices begin to change. The male hormone enlarges the cartilage and muscles of the voice box. During this growth, a boy's voice can sound warbly and often may crack.

Your son's skin will begin to change, too. The oil glands become more active, which can lead to skin problems like pimples and acne. Sweat glands, also in the skin, start to produce more body odor.

Girls Becoming Women

Girls today are maturing earlier than girls in previous generations. The onset of puberty usually occurs about two years earlier for girls than for boys, somewhere between the ages of 8 and 18 years. The average age for a girl to have her first period is now just under 13 years.

Usually, a girl's puberty lasts about four years. The first sign your daughter may notice is the growth of pubic hair, then underarm hair. At the same time—usually about the age of 11 or 12—she'll notice that her breasts are beginning to grow.

Breasts start with a breast bud, or a little bump under the nipple. One breast may bud before the other. Be sure to reassure your daughter that uneven growth is normal, and that both breasts soon will be approximately the same size. If her breasts are tender and hurt a bit, tell her that's also normal. If she complains of pain rather than discomfort,

Of Pads and Tampons

At about the time your daughter's breasts show signs of developing, it's time to stock up on supplies for her soon-arriving period.

But what to purchase? Sanitary pads certainly do the job. But some girls find them uncomfortable.

Many young women prefer tampons. That's fine. But be aware that tampon use has been linked to toxic shock syndrome—a rare but sometimes fatal disease that happens primarily to girls and young women.

In order to reduce the risk, your daughter should follow these rules:

- Always wash hands before inserting the tampon.

- Remove the tampon after 4 to 6 hours and replace it with a fresh one.

- Use a sanitary pad overnight.

delayed puberty

 f your daughter is between 12 and 13, or your son is between 14 and 15, and he or she is exceptionally short, you may be looking at a case of delayed puberty.

Clearly, each teenager's growth is different. Some mature later than others, and they are well within the range of normal. But about one child in 100 (or about 1 percent) is significantly slow to mature.

Such adolescents are short for their age because they have continued to grow at the same, slower rate of childhood. They don't get the same adolescent growth spurt that their peers experience. They also show no sign of developing any sexual characteristics.

If you are concerned about your teen's progress, schedule a visit to the doctor. The doctor may

Mom, my girlfriends are hanging out with some of the older kids in school, and they tease me when I hang out with them. They call me pip-squeak and stuff like that. Is there something wrong with me? Why am I so small?

Kids your age grow at all different speeds. There's nothing wrong with you. I'm afraid your friends aren't treating you fairly. Instead of hanging out with your friends, how about taking a bike ride with the family this weekend?

take X rays, which can show whether the bones are maturing at a slower rate than most kids of your teen's age—a sure sign of delayed puberty.

What causes delayed puberty? Sometimes chronic illness, malnutrition—even stress—can create a problem. But, in most cases, the cause is unknown.

Kids with delayed puberty will catch up to their peers eventually. They'll be just as tall and just as attractive to the opposite sex. In the meantime, however, they can be miserable. They're called Shorty or Shrimp. They're excluded from boy-girl parties. They feel inadequate and left out. At this time of their lives, feeling rejected is particularly rough.

In this time of waiting for the growth spurt, you must be especially supportive of your son or daughter. Explain that puberty surely will come, that it's just a matter of time.

Try to take up some of the social slack by spending more time with your teenager. Go to the movies together, go shopping, ride your bikes to the park. Whatever activity you choose, make the experience upbeat.

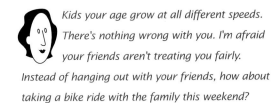

Kids with delayed puberty will catch up to their peers eventually. They'll be just as tall, and just as attractive to the opposite sex.

Also talk to your teen's doctor. Several studies have shown that the experimental drug oxandrolone (similar to testosterone) can help boys with delayed puberty to grow a little faster. Soon they are as tall as their peers.

Doctors sometimes suggest stimulating sexual development with sex hormones—testosterone for boys, and estrogen (or estrogen and progestin combos) for girls.

Hormones usually are given for a limited time—about six months to a year. Low doses do not appear to affect the teenager's final adult height.

however, talk to your doctor. Also consult your doctor if your daughter's breasts have not started to develop by age 14, especially if she seems concerned about slow maturation.

You'll also notice that your daughter is beginning to get a little wider through the hips and narrower in the waist. And the vulva will enlarge. All of these changes are accompanied by a spurt in both height and weight.

Girls, in fact, do not simply gain weight. Their body composition—the ratio of fat to lean—also changes. A young girl's body is about 16 percent fat. As she matures, her body will come to be composed of about 27 percent fat.

It's not that the lean, muscular tissue somehow turns into fat. Not at all. During puberty, girls are still gaining muscle. They are simply gaining fat tissue faster. This change in body composition is necessary to menstruate and to reproduce.

Menstruation is a new experience. Your daughter will have no gauge against which to measure what is normal and what may signal a problem. Make it a point to be available for talking about this new experience.

Once her body shows signs of body hair and breast development, your daughter is close to menarche—the beginning of the menstrual period. In fact, menstruation usually starts about two years after breast development has begun, and about one year after your daughter's growth spurt.

Researchers theorize that the timing of the first period is somehow related to the amount of body fat your daughter has. Girls who do not have enough body fat do not get their periods as early as girls who do. When a girl starts to menstruate, it means she is (or soon will be) capable of having a baby. If your daughter has not started to menstruate by the age of 16, you may want to consult your doctor.

The first few periods usually are "anovulatory," which means ovulation has not occurred. For that reason, their timing can be a little off. In fact, during the first months of menstruation your daughter may miss a period altogether.

Menstruation is a new experience for your daughter. She will have no gauge against which to measure what is normal and what may signal a problem. Make it

Menstruation: What to Tell Your Daughter At some point before The Big Day arrives, you will want to talk to your daughter about what it is like to menstruate and to help her understand what to expect. Don't wait until the last minute. If you haven't discussed it before, make sure you bring it up as soon as your daughter shows her first signs of entering puberty. Begin with the basics.

Tell her that each month she will get her period. The menstrual cycle is measured from the first day of the period to the first day of her next period. The length of cycles is different for every girl. The average cycle is 28 days, but anywhere from 21 to 45 days is normal. Periods do not always arrive exactly on time, especially at first. Explain to your daughter that it will be more convenient (and tons less embarrassing) if she is prepared for her period a few days before its expected ▶

a point, then, to be available for talking about this new experience.

Tell your daughter that, when a girl is menstruating, she may feel tired or irritable right before her period. She also may have some abdominal cramps. Suggest a little exercise or a hot bath, which sometimes helps. Products like Advil and Motrin also ease the pain. However, some girls get very painful cramps and may need medical attention or medication to relieve the discomfort. It's always appropriate to talk to a doctor about anything that raises concerns for either you or your daughter.

Seeing the Doctor

Most teenagers are healthy as horses, so—unless they break a bone or need a doctor's okay to join a sports team—they can go a long time between doctor visits. And, in these days of managed health care, the yearly physical is not encouraged. "But, in my personal opinion," says Dr. Karver, "I think an annual visit is a good idea. We can review what has happened in the past year, as well as check the child's weight and blood pressure. In addition, we can keep inoculations current."

As for inoculation scheduling, the recommendations change so frequently that it's best to ask your doctor about which shots should be given at specific ages. At this writing, it's suggested that boosters of diphtheria and tetanus be given every ten years; and an MMR shot (measles, mumps, and rubella) at 14 to 16 years.

Besides the annual check-up, sometimes girls need additional care. For example, if a teenage girl becomes sexually active, she should see her family doctor or a gynecologist for a pelvic examination. "This is also a good time to talk about birth control," says Dr. Karver. If a girl is sexually active and misses her period, she also should see a doctor at once. For more details on how to deal with your teen's developing sexuality, see "Dating and Sexuality" on page 102.

The teenage years are a time when some kids prefer to switch from a pediatrician to a specialist in adolescent health or to a family practitioner. Usually, preteens and young teens are fine with going to the pediatrician. However, when they approach the mid- to late-teens, they begin to feel like Gulliver in the Land of Lilliput. Sitting in the waiting room besides mommies and their tiny tots can get under a teenager's skin. The day will come when your son or daughter will be ready to move on.

◄ arrival. That means either taking a sanitary pad or tampon to school, or having the right change for the dispenser in the Girls' Room. Explain to your daughter that she will get her period about 10 days after an egg cell produced by one of the ovaries matures and begins to travel down the fallopian tube toward the uterus.

This pear-shaped organ is where a baby grows during pregnancy. The lining of the uterus thickens and prepares for pregnancy. If the egg is not fertilized by a male sperm, this lining is not needed. The uterus contracts and both the egg and lining pass out of the uterus through the vagina. This monthly bleeding lasts about five days. The flow is usually heaviest on the first or second day. Suggest that your daughter pay special attention to personal hygiene during her period. Just as perspiration has an odor, so does menstrual flow. She'll need to shower every day and change sanitary napkins or tampons frequently.

2

feed me

Teens grow at an enormous rate. This growth spurt requires the right kind of food ... and lots of it.

between Jeffrey's 14th and 15th birthdays, he grew 12 inches, shooting up from only 5 feet tall to a manly 6 feet. His growth was so rapid that he looks elongated and ungainly—all elbows, knees, and Adam's apple.

"How can he be so skinny?" his mother wonders. "He eats us out of house and home!"

A growth spurt like Jeffrey's requires an immense amount of food. His body hungers for protein to build tissue and muscle, calcium to strengthen and lengthen bones, iron to support the increasing volume of the blood in his veins—and MORE, much more.

Meanwhile, Maureen has reached her adult height at age 15. But, unlike Jeffrey, she has grown slowly and steadily over a longer period of time. Even so, her nutritional needs are proportionately as great as his. In one specific way, in fact, they are greater.

Because she has reached puberty and has begun experiencing her monthly period, she needs a significant amount of iron.

Building the Future

Good nutrition is important to teenagers for many reasons. But the most important of all is that what they eat today affects their bodies tomorrow and all through their future. Slender or plump, strong boned or weak, what your teenager turns into in the future starts with eating habits learned in childhood. A good diet, moreover, can help prevent several serious diseases that are quite common in

Tell them that a good diet will help them feel more energetic, earn better grades, and be both more attractive and more popular.

older adults. Heart disease, high blood pressure, diabetes, stroke, osteoporosis, some types of cancer—all have been linked to a person's lifetime diet.

Teenagers (indestructible and immortal, or so they believe) will not forgo their bacon cheeseburgers based on some vague benefit promised for their unthinkable and far-off old age. So, don't waste your breath on these arguments.

Yet, as a responsible parent, you have to convince your teen that a good diet really does matter. So, what should parents tell their sons and daughters?

Tell them the truth—but a truth they can relate to. Tell them that a good diet will help them feel more energetic, earn better grades, and be both more attractive and more popular. (Good-looking, successful "doers" seem to attract friends automatically!)

Nutrition Basics

What do teenagers need from food? Calories. And, for most kids, lots of them! Calories provide them with energy to study, play ball, run for the school bus, bike to a friend's house, learn the latest dance, crawl the mall, and all the other great and silly things they do each day.

Yet, even in these growth years, teens must be taught to be aware of how much they are eating. Their calorie needs vary by their age and level of activity. Clearly, a cerebral 12-year-old with an Internet addiction simply doesn't need as much food as his 16-year-old sister who runs cross-country track. And student athletes in a training program may consume—and use up—3,000 or more calories a day.

For kids who mostly sit—sit in class, sit in front of the TV or computer—counting calories and/or exercising is the only way to avoid becoming fat. For these kids, low-fat meals and low-cal snacks are important. (For more on dealing with excess weight, see Overweight on page 130.)

Of course, not just any calories will do. The calories your kids consume

How Many Calories Your Teen Should Eat

Boys

11–14 years	2,500
15–18 years	3,000

Girls

11–14 years	2,200
15–18 years	2,200

breaking the fast really fast

helen L. Miller asked her tenth grade homeroom, "How many of you ate breakfast this morning?" She saw only a smattering of hands.

Undaunted, the home economics teacher asked her standard follow-up question: "How many of you would like to eat breakfast?" Every hand rose.

Miller isn't teaching in some third world nation where war or natural disaster led to famine. Oh, no. She teaches in an affluent New Jersey suburb. And the kids in Williamstown High School are no different than their peers across the nation. They'd rather spend that extra 15 minutes in bed than get up to deal with breakfast.

The end result? Kids running on empty. Kids who do not learn well. Medical research has shown time and time again that they don't remember their lessons. They're inattentive. Listless. And they're cranky.

> "You don't even have to be home for your kids to have either a nourishing breakfast or a healthy snack after school."

Grab It & Go

You can lick the problem with a healthy, delicious meal—one that will get your kid's day off to a strong start. What? You say that you barely have time to gulp down a cup of coffee for yourself? How are you to prepare a delicious meal?

"It's all in the planning," says Anita Hirsch, R.D., nutrition counselor and food columnist in Allentown, Pennsylvania. "You don't even have to be home for your kids to have either a nourishing breakfast or a healthy snack after school."

The Cache in the Cabinet   Just in case the kids actually have time to sit down to eat, load up the cabinet with breakfast cereals. All are vitamin fortified and can fill in vitamins that teens may be missing, such as vitamins B6 and C, and the minerals iron, calcium, and zinc.

The Delicious Drawer   Also stock the drawer with food items that most teenagers find acceptable: oatmeal raisin cookies, peanut butter crackers, whole wheat crackers (preferably the reduced-fat version), a mix of peanuts and raisins, little cans of water-packed tuna, and single servings of canned fruit.

The 'Raid Me First' Fridge   "In the refrigerator," says Hirsch, "leave them some low-fat mozzarella sticks, some cut-up oranges in a plastic baggie, ready-made puddings, instant breakfast in cans, cubes of cheese, and some bran or blueberry muffins. If your kids are adventurous with food, you might also stock some hummus and pita bread. Or buy a big submarine sandwich—say, turkey, cheese, and vegetables—slice it, and wrap up small individual portions," says Hirsch. "Or, you can prepare a little extra for dinner and save it in a margarine tub. Kids will eat a breakfast of cold macaroni and cheese or a slice of leftover meatloaf," she says.

Some Frozen Assets   "Next, stock the freezer with some green grapes, some peeled bananas wrapped in cling-film, and some low-fat frozen yogurt," Hirsch suggests.

While not all of these foods are nutritionally perfect, they are all good. They'll give the kids the boost they need to start the school day right. And, says Hirsch, "They are 'peer acceptable.'"

should be loaded with carbohydrates, proteins, vitamins, and minerals. And that means eating real food. The calories from soda or candy, for example, are called "empty calories" because they provide little nutrition.

Carbohydrates, fats, and proteins are measured in calories. Carbs and proteins provide about 4 calories per gram. Fat contributes more than twice that amount—about 9 calories a gram. (Maybe that's why it's called fat!)

All these food elements provide the essential vitamins and minerals your children need. A healthy diet contains the nutrients and calories needed to prevent nutritional deficiencies. It provides the right balance of carbohydrate, fat, and protein to help your kids achieve their peak potential.

Your teens, now making many food decisions on their own, need real guidance from you. They should be encouraged to make sensible food choices. Parents cannot assume that school lunches provide sound nutrition. (After all, salsa has been declared a "vegetable" in the federal school lunch program.) Nor can parents assume that the vending machines in school lobbies and cafeterias are stocked with cold fresh fruit. While some are, most sell those bright and appealing little packages of chips and candy bars.

How to Read a Nutrition Label

It's hard to believe, but true, that those colorful labels on packaged foods are more than just eye-catching. They're loaded with information that can help you to make wise food choices.

Pick up a can of whole-kernel sweet corn, for example. On the back, you'll find a box that gives you all the vital statistics. It begins by telling you that the can contains a little more than 3 servings, and that each serving is ½ cup or 121 grams.

Right at the top of the box, the label will tell you how many calories are in each serving, and how many of those calories come from fat. Next, it reveals what used to be a dirty little secret—the amount of total fat in a serving. In the case of this can of corn, the amount is a very modest 0.5 grams.

The label then tells you how much of that total fat is saturated fat, and how much cholesterol is in each serving. The next listing is for sodium content. Here our corn registers 180 milligrams. The label then gives you relevant data on carbohydrates: the total amount in grams, dietary fiber in grams, and sugar—also in grams.

The label finishes up with the amount of protein, in grams. Each line also tells you what percentage of your daily requirement will be met. The listing is called Percent Daily Value, and the values are based on a 2,000-calorie-a-day diet. This serving of corn, for example, provides 6 percent of our daily carbohydrate value.

By reading food labels, you can weed out products high in saturated fat or

Recommended Dietary Allowances for Adolescent Boys	
11 to 14 years	
protein, grams	45
Vitamin A, IU	5,000
Vitamin D, IU	400
Vitamin E , IU	10
Vitamin K, mcg	45
Vitamin C, mg	50
Thiamine, mg	1.3
Riboflavin, mg	1.5
Niacin, mg	17
Vitamin B6, mg	1.7
Folate, mcg	150
Vitamin B12, mcg	2
Calcium, mg	1,200
Phosphorus, mg	1,200
Magnesium mg	270
Iron, mg	12
Zinc, mg	15
Iodine, mcg	150
Selenium, mcg	40
15 to 18 years	
protein, grams	59
Vitamin A, IU	5,000
Vitamin D, IU	400
Vitamin E, IU	10
Vitamin K, mcg	65
Vitamin C, mg	60
Thiamine, mg	1.5
Riboflavin, mg	1.8
Niacin, mg	20
Vitamin B6, mg	2
Folate, mcg	200
Vitamin B12, mcg	2
Calcium. mg	1,200
Phosphorus, mg	1,200
Magnesium, mg	400
Iron, mg	12
Zinc, mg	15
Iodine, mcg	150
Selenium, mcg	50

sodium, and select those that will provide the highest percentage of nutrition per serving. Both of these concerns are important for growing teenagers.

The Balancing Act

Let's take a look at some typical American dinners. Here's what you might find on tables across the nation tonight:

- Hamburgers
- Fried chicken with biscuits
- Stuffed pork chops with gravy
- Roast beef and mashed potatoes
- Veal parmigiana

Notice the way each meal is defined by the meat being served. Nutritionists and dietitians say we must change our focus on making meat the center of a meal. Sure, meat provides lots of protein, B vitamins, and minerals. But often it also lays on the fat.

Experts suggest that you shove meat aside and put grains at the center of the plate.

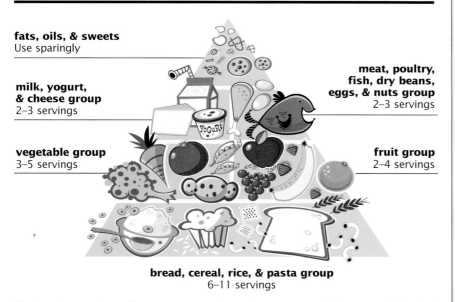

fats, oils, & sweets
Use sparingly

milk, yogurt, & cheese group
2–3 servings

vegetable group
3–5 servings

meat, poultry, fish, dry beans, eggs, & nuts group
2–3 servings

fruit group
2–4 servings

bread, cereal, rice, & pasta group
6–11 servings

Note: The number of servings varies depending on your kids' size and level of activity. The low number is for the smaller and/or less active child. The large number is for the big, very active kid. Most teens' servings requirements falls in between.

Recommended Dietary Allowances for Adolescent Girls

11 to 14 years

protein, grams	46
Vitamin A, IU	4,000
Vitamin D, IU	400
Vitamin E, mg	8
Vitamin K, mcg	45
Vitamin C, mg	50
Thiamine, mg	1.1
Riboflavin, mg	1.3
Niacin, mg	15
Vitamin B6, mg	1.4
Folate, mcg	150
Vitamin B12, mcg	2
Calcium, mg	1,200
Phosphorus, mg	1,200
Magnesium, mg	280
Iron, mg	15
Zinc, mg	12
Iodine, mcg	150
Selenium, mcg	45

15 to 18 years

protein, grams	44
Vitamin A, IU	4,000
Vitamin D, IU	400
Vitamin E, mg	8
Vitamin K, mcg	55
Vitamin C, mg	60
Thiamine, mg	1.1
Riboflavin, mg	1.3
Niacin, mg	15
Vitamin B6, mg	1.5
Folate, mcg	180
Vitamin B12, mcg	2
Calcium, mg	1,200
Phosphorus, mg	1,200
Magnesium, mg	300
Iron, mg	15
Zinc, mg	12
Iodine, mcg	150
Selenium, mcg	50

Using the Food Guide Pyramid, you'll see that the U.S. Department of Agriculture suggests you make bread, cereal, grains, and pasta the basis of your diet. Plan on feeding your kids six to 11 servings a day. Next, offer three to five servings of vegetables each day, and two to four servings of fruit. Include two to three servings of meat, poultry, fish, dry beans, eggs, and nuts. Provide at least two to three servings of dairy food each day—milk, cheese, and yogurt. Finally, offer small amounts of fats (usually butter or margarine), oils (usually for frying or in salad dressing), and sweets.

Gains from Grains

There are different approaches you might take to making an adjustment to eating more grains. One way is to go grain gourmet, creating dishes such as Risotto Romano or Paella Valenciana, and the like. But the chances are, your kids will be wary of such exotic fare.

Instead, make sure the kids load up on grains in more ordinary—and easier—ways.

For breakfast: give them cereal and toast in the morning, or a sturdy pile of waffles or pancakes.

For lunch: fix sandwiches on big kaiser or hoagie rolls.

For dinner: serve pasta frequently. Concoct side dishes that combine rice (or any other grain) with the vegetables and herbs you know your kids like. And serve dinner with delicious whole grain rolls, garlic bread, or a crusty French baguette.

Broccoli Battles and Other Skirmishes

The real key to ensuring a healthy diet for your teen is to provide a variety of foods. Vegetables and fruits also are essential elements of a varied diet. They provide vitamins, minerals, and complex carbohydrates (starch and dietary fiber). And they're usually low in fat! Unfortunately, many kids eat fewer than the recommended number of servings of these foods. (Although some teens will argue that a bag of chips "is, too, a serving of vegetables," or that strawberry gelatin is really fruit.)

So be sure to provide your kids with plenty of vegetables and fruits. And avoid the trap of pushing some vegetables over others. It is true that broccoli is nutritionally superior to, say, cucumbers. But if your kids hate broccoli, but will eat cucumbers—well, as Marie Antoinette might have said, "Let them eat cukes."

Most teenagers will gladly dig into potatoes, sweet potatoes, carrots, corn, tomatoes, and other sweet or mild-tasting vegetables. Just make sure that, over the span of a few days, they eat a variety.

Meat in Moderation

Because teenagers are growing so quickly, they need to eat meat and/or other foods in the meat group—fish, poultry, eggs, peas, and beans. Nutritionists recommend that teenage girls eat two servings each day from the meat group, for a total of 6 ounces. Teenage boys should have three helpings from the meat group, for a total of 7 ounces.

Select lean cuts of meat, and then remove any visible fat. When you cook chicken, first remove the skin. Also try to limit the amount of high-fat processed meat that you buy—such as sausages, salami, and other cold cuts. When buying packaged meat, be sure to read the Nutrition Facts

What Makes a Serving?

Is a mixing bowl full of cereal considered one serving? Is a rice cake also one serving? Here's a rundown of what counts as a serving in each of the five food groups.

Grains
1   slice of bread
1   ounce of ready-to-eat cereal
½   cup of cooked cereal, rice, or pasta

Vegetables
1   cup of raw, leafy vegetables
½   cup of any other vegetable, cooked or raw
6   ounces of vegetable juice

Fruits
1   medium apple, banana, or orange
½   cup of chopped, cooked, or canned fruit
6   ounces of fruit juice

Dairy
1   cup of milk or yogurt
1½ ounces of natural cheese
2   ounces of processed cheese

Meat and Beans
2–3 ounces of cooked lean meat, poultry, or fish
½   cup of cooked dry beans
1   egg
2   Tbsp. peanut butter
⅓   cup nuts

snacking for fiber

Snacks can provide a large percentage of a teenager's daily calories, so it's important that you provide the right stuff. The occasional ice cream float or bag of chips is inevitable. But the mainstays of your snack menu should be grains, fruits, and even raw vegetables.

In addition to being low in calories and high in nutrition, fruit, veggie, and grain snacks can provide lots of beneficial fiber.

Fiber, itself, is not a nutrient. However, it affects the way the body absorbs nutrients.

Fiber adds bulk to the diet and helps to relieve constipation. It may bind to cholesterol and flush it from the body—thus lowering the long-term risk of heart disease. And it speeds up digestion.

These snacks also are excellent for teens who are watching their weight. Foods high in fiber, the experts say, fill you up without filling you out.

> **Fiber, itself, is not a nutrient. However, it affects the way the body absorbs nutrients.**

Food	Serving	Fiber (in grams)
apple	1 small	3.1
carrot sticks	1 carrot	3.7
celery, raw	2½ stalks	3.0
graham crackers	2 squares	1.5
grapefruit	½	2.6
orange	1 small	1.8
peaches, canned	½ cup	1.3
strawberries	½ cup	2.6
whole wheat bread	1 slice	2.4

Label on the package so that you can select the most nutritious brand.

Adolescents' growing bodies need meat because of its iron content. This mineral is vital because of the expanding volume of blood in that growing body. Plus, daughters are at some risk of deficiency because of the amount of iron lost through menstruation. A few nutritional surveys have shown that the average American diet doesn't contain enough iron to meet the demands of puberty.

Because teenagers are growing so quickly, they need to eat meat and/or other foods in the meat group—fish, poultry, eggs, peas, and beans.

A possible result of eating a diet low in this mineral is iron-deficiency anemia. This condition occurs when the body does not get enough iron to manufacture hemoglobin, the substance in the blood that carries life-giving oxygen to the cells throughout the body. The symptoms of iron-deficiency anemia develop slowly. One of the earliest symptoms of this condition is fatigue, especially after exercising. If the anemia becomes more serious, you'll notice that your teen looks pale and perhaps has cracking of the skin at the corners of the mouth.

Fortunately, this type of anemia is easily diagnosed with a blood test and also is easily remedied, not only with a good diet but often with iron supplements. (Do not give your teenager iron supplements unless a doctor tells you to do so.)

A Case for Dairy Food

Teenagers need substantial amounts of calcium to support their growing bones. In fact, both boys and girls in their teen years require 1,200 milligrams of calcium every day. Meeting that requirement means drinking milk and eating dairy foods like cheeses and yogurt.

One 8-ounce glass of milk provides 255 milligrams of calcium. Therefore, your child can meet his or her requirement by drinking four glasses (1 quart) of milk a day. And that's a fine and easy way to provide sufficient calcium.

Go for skim. If your child tends to be heavy, consider buying only skim milk or low-fat milk to cut down on calories.

Think soup. If your child doesn't like milk, try making creamed soups (tomato bisque, New England clam chowder, or cream of celery, for example). Stock up on pudding made with milk, as well as low-fat cheese and fruited yogurt. Or offer lots of nondairy foods high in calcium, such as broccoli, soybeans, turnip greens, almonds, and canned fish such as sardines and salmon. (The calcium is in the tiny bones, which should always be consumed.)

Help that digestion. If your teen has lactose intolerance—the inability to digest milk and dairy products—buy acidophilus milk, or add a product such as Lactaid to regular milk.

Keep Fat to a Pat

Most doctors recommend that a diet should contain no more than 30 percent of calories from fat. They make this recommendation because a diet that contains more than 30 percent of fat can lead to high cholesterol (yes, even in teens!), obesity, and an increased risk of heart disease in the future.

The greatest risk comes from eating saturated fats, which should be kept to only 10 percent of the daily diet. These are found mostly in meat, milk, and milk products.

To keep saturated fat levels down, consider switching to low-fat or no-fat dairy products. The remaining fat calories should be made up of vegetable oils, specifically olive oil and canola oil. These are called monounsaturated fats. Polyunsaturated fats—found in most other vegetable oils, such as corn and safflower oil—can complete the picture.

Ten Easy Ways to Limit Fat

1 Toss out the fry pan. Instead, broil or steam your food.

2 Switch to skim milk and low-fat dairy products.

3 Read the Nutrition Facts Label of packaged food to select products with the lowest amount of fat per serving. (Look for the line that says, "Total calories from Fat...")

4 Use fat-free salad dressing and low-fat mayonnaise.

5 Dress your veggies with herbs, spices, or lemon juice rather than butter.

6 Buy only lean cuts of meat, poultry, and fish, then trim away any visible fat.

7 Remove the skin from chicken.

8 Once a week (or more frequently) substitute beans or tofu for meat.

9 Don't buy cold cuts, salami, bacon, or sausages.

10 Use a frozen scrambled "egg" product, or egg whites, in place of whole eggs.

Mom, I won't eat meat

I t's a girl thing, mostly. One day your daughter (or your son), while setting the dinner table, announces, "Mom, I just can't eat anything that has a face!"

Girls like to experiment with vegetarian diets. For one thing, these diets generally cause some weight loss. For another, girls who won't eat "anything with a face" can take the moral high ground—a much-valued spot in the teen years—and peer down upon their cruelly carnivorous parents.

If your child decides to trade her burger for a slice of grilled eggplant, that's fine. But be aware that meat, fish, and poultry are major contributors of iron, zinc, and B vitamins. You'll have to keep careful watch that your daughter is filling her nutritional requirements in other ways. Also be sure that she's consuming enough calories to fuel her active lifestyle, enough calcium for strong bones, and enough protein for tissue growth and repair.

Most vegetarians eat milk products and eggs. They're called lacto-ovo vegetarians. If your child elects to follow this diet, it will be relatively easy for her to fill her nutritional needs. Steer your daughter toward low-fat dairy products. And encourage her to eat fortified bread and breakfast cereal to fill her iron requirement.

Some vegetarians, however, are vegans—people who also exclude dairy and egg products from their diet. Meeting the nutritional needs of a growing adolescent on a vegan diet can be difficult. But it can be done.

The biggest concern for vegans is getting vitamin B12, which is found only in animal foods. The sign of a deficiency of this vitamin is a red tongue that has a smoother than normal surface. The easy solution is to take a multivitamin and mineral supplement.

Also of concern is meeting the calcium requirement. Without dairy products, you'll have to

> **You'll have to keep careful watch that your daughter is filling her nutritional requirements in other ways.**

Mom, I just don't think it's right. I mean, cows have mothers too, you know. Besides, all that meat, cheese, and eggs are making me fat. I want to lose weight, so from now on I'm only eating salads.

Well, if you want to be a vegetarian that's your decision, but there's more to being a vegetarian than eating salads. There are certain nutrients that you need to make sure you're getting. Let's sit down and work out a menu for you.

---

make your child aware of the importance of eating green, leafy vegetables; chick peas; figs; black-strap molasses; oranges; broccoli; navy beans; nuts, such as brazil nuts, almonds, and filberts; and soy products, such as tofu. Also consider buying orange juice with added calcium.

To be sure your kid is getting enough iron, stock up on high-iron foods like enriched grains, legumes, dried fruits, and vegetables, such as broccoli, kale, and collards. Also, be sure to serve a food high in vitamin C along with an iron-rich food. This vitamin helps the body to better absorb and use iron. Your young vegan will be happy with citrus fruits as part of her morning meals. And she'll most likely welcome sweet peppers, onions, and tomatoes with her dinner.

3

they're growing up

What do *you* do? One moment they love you. In the next, World War III explodes in your face. What's going on here?

teenagers are creatures of great contradictions. At one moment, they are testing limits and experimenting with independence. The next, they are seeking closeness with and reassurance from their parents that they are still loved and valued members of the family. Adolescence can also be a time of great loneliness, a sense that no one has ever before experienced such a miserable state of being. Yet it is also a time of intense peer activity and expanding interpersonal relationships.

The teen years also a time of frequent assertions of self-assuredness, as adolescents seek increased autonomy in decision-making. But these years are a time when adolescents experience tremendous doubt that they can, in fact, go it alone.

These many contradictions—the "push and pull" of adolescence—are the inevitable result of the primary task of the teenage years: to achieve a sense of personal identity separate from parents. This search for identity, as noted author and psychologist Erik Erikson described it, is a struggle to know who they are, what they believe in and value, and what they want to accomplish and get out of life. The outcome of this search is neither certain nor easy. So have patience with your teen.

Making this struggle especially pressing is the fact that soon—very soon—they will be leaving home and on their own. Despite the bravado of adolescents, deep down, many teenagers are more than just a little bit frightened by the prospect. So they are constantly testing themselves to see how much of life they can handle on their own.

This search for identity is a struggle to know who they are, what they believe in, and what they want to accomplish and get out of life.

In this respect, the teenage years are really a more mature version of the terrible twos. The reason that 2- and 3-year-olds can be so frustrating to parents is that they are trying to determine just how capable they really are. "Let me do it!" is the frequent cry of the two-year-old struggling to put his or her shirt on right side forward.

Teenagers may be confident that they can put their shirt on correctly (although most still don't seem to understand in which direction a baseball cap is supposed to go), but are often less self-assured when it comes to handling more mature expressions of independence and autonomy from Mom and Dad, such as how to resist peer pressure to use alcohol or illegal drugs.

From this struggle between independence and autonomy on the one hand and dependence and a desire for family affiliation on the other, flow two important consequences: first, a reticence to seek advice from one's parents, and second, an increase in risk-taking behavior.

My Teenager, the Clam!

One of the most remarkable transformations undertaken by the human species happens when our young enter the teenage years. They suddenly become clams!

Oh, not all the time, of course. The very same teenager who can spend hours on the phone talking with friends about such engrossing topics as their latest lipstick

The Best Laid Plans ... One of the authors of this book (Wade Horn) learned just how unpredictable communication can be with teens when several years ago his then 15-year-old daughter came to him with a request. She wanted him to help her buy two tickets to a Dave Matthews Band concert. Why? She wanted to give him one of the tickets as a Father's Day gift.

For several days afterwards, he walked around on cloud nine. His teenage daughter wanted to take her dear old dad to a rock concert! How much more hip can a father-daughter relationship get!

Then, after the tickets arrived, she sheepishly asked whether it would be OK with him if she used his ticket to go

color or last night's basketball game often seems incapable of any verbalization with a parent beyond the occasional (and often begrudging) grunt. Why?

Could it be that all your earlier admonitions that "silence is golden" and "children should be seen, but not heard" have come back to haunt you? Not likely. The real reason so many teenagers go mute around their parents is that seeking advice and counsel from them is incompatible with discovering just how much they can do for themselves. Two-year-olds do this with their loud cries of "Let me do it!" Teenagers assert their independence through silence.

The same child who used to ask you incessant questions like, "Why is the sky blue?" and "Why is your bedroom door locked?" now frequently goes mute whenever asked a question as complicated as "How was your day?"

This doesn't mean that you will never have good conversations with your teenagers. You will. Teens and their parents spend some part of their time getting along with each other very nicely, sharing new experiences, talking over plans and problems, and just plain enjoying each other's company. But usually these conversations happen on their timetable, not yours. Teenagers talk to us when they want to, not necessarily when we want them to.

In this respect, communication with teenagers is like a roller-coaster ride. Sometimes you're hot, and sometimes you're not. You need to roll with the punches. You gotta go with the flow... Oh, you get the idea.

Breaking Through

The point is that communication with teenagers can be both spotty and unpredictable. The fact that teenagers do not respond to every parental overture with hours of discussion does not mean that we should stop making overtures. Teenagers need to know that despite their unwillingness to talk to us, we are always willing to listen to them. The worst thing parents can do is to respond to their teenager's silence with silence of their own.

Communicate your love. It is especially important during the teenage years for parents to go out of their way to let their teenagers know—every day, and in a myriad of ways—how precious they are to us and how deeply we care about and love them. Teens need to know that in a pinch, you will be there—that no matter what happens, you are on their side. If you get this message across, you can rest easier

with a friend instead (a boy, no less!). Working quickly through his disappointment, he came up with what he thought was a cunning plan. He told her that despite the fact that she had asked to buy the tickets with one plan in mind, and that he was looking forward to going to the concert with her, he was not going to make this decision for her. Instead, he told her she should "talk this one over with God" and that together she and God should come to a conclusion.

Several days later, she approached him again. "Dad," she began, "I did what you said, and talked this whole thing over with God." Ah, hah, he thought, his planned worked! But before he could complete his mental victory dance, she added, "And God and I both feel real bad for you..."

knowing that if your kids do get into trouble, they'll turn to you for help.

Don't ignore warning signs. There are exceptions, of course. If your teenager's noncommunicativeness is combined with a loss of appetite, a sudden and marked drop in grades, or difficulty taking care of their daily activities, it could be a signal of depression, drug use, or other emotional problems. In such cases, you should consult with a qualified mental health expert.

But most of the time, the moodiness and noncommunicativeness of teenagers just comes with the territory. If you were expecting to spend hours each evening in deep conversation with your teenager, sharing your feelings with one another, and ending each intimate session with a hug and a good cry, well, good luck. Just keep in mind that when your teenager grunts at you, what he or she is really saying is, "I can do it myself." At least he or she wants to try.

Differences Between Male And Female Teens

Just as there are differences between younger and older teens, there are also differences between male and female teens. Here are some of the most prominent differences:

Girls

Emphasize intimacy and emotional support more frequently in their friendships

Report higher levels of social anxiety, especially fears of social rejection

Are more concerned about others' judgments of their appearance and behavior

Evidence more depression and anxiety

Boys

Have more health risk behaviors, like smoking, drinking, and illicit drug use

Engage in more high-risk behaviors resulting in more physical injuries

Are more accepting of theft, lying, and fighting

Evidence more conduct problems

In other words... When boys are stressed, they are more likely to act out and engage in high-risk behaviors involving physical violence and aggression. When girls are stressed, they are more likely to turn that stress inward and become depressed and anxious.

The Second Coming of Evel Knievel

The second consequence of a teenager's struggle with dependence and independence is a rapid rise in risk-taking behavior. For some, risk taking takes the form of pursuing new interests, trying on new clothing, experimenting with hairstyles, and getting that first real job. For others, it can mean drinking, smoking, drug use, criminal behavior, violence, and sexual activity.

The reason teenagers engage in risk-taking behavior is that it's one way to demonstrate to themselves that they are capable, grown up, and independent from their parents. Of course, they aren't really. Which is why you are still necessary. It is your job to set limits on your teens' risk taking and steer them toward age-appropriate ways of experimenting with their newfound desire for autonomy.

The daughter of one of the authors of this book (Wade Horn), for example, once insisted that it was perfectly reasonable to walk a couple of miles to a friend's house in a blinding snowstorm—a snowstorm which was later described as the "snowstorm of the century." That particular weekend her grandfather was baby-sitting, and he let her go. Even she later admitted it was a pretty foolish thing to do.

This illustrates two things: First, teens often have trouble foreseeing just how dangerous a particular behavior can be. Second, never let a grandfather who has suffered a couple of mild strokes baby-sit your teenager during the "snowstorm of the century."

Risk taking in adolescence is especially dangerous because teenagers often have a sense of invincibility. While acknowledging that some behaviors can be risky, teenagers frequently say to themselves, "But it won't happen to me."

So teenagers begin smoking cigarettes because "I won't get hooked." Or they

The reason teenagers engage in risk-taking behavior is that it's one way to demonstrate to themselves that they are capable, grown up, and independent from their parents.

experiment with sex because "Pregnancy can't happen to me."

Take, for example, one common area of risk taking that can have very tragic consequences: reckless driving. Each year, motor vehicle accidents account for

stress and teenagers

adolescence is stressful. Some of the things that cause stress are external to the family—peers, school, and the broader community. Other stressors are internal to the family—parental conflict or divorce, parental depression or physical health problems, and parent-child conflict. Still others are inherent—such as the teen's own temperament.

It is not so much the type of stressor that causes problems, but the number of stressors. Research suggests that most adolescents can cope with one, two, or even three stressors, provided none are especially severe or prolonged. When four or more stressors coexist, however, teens can get into real trouble. They may, for example, develop problems in school, behavior problems, or psychiatric disorders.

On the other hand, it's not good for teens to experience no stress during adolescence. It is only through experiencing challenges and overcoming them that teens develop confidence in their ability to do so.

In fact, stress can help living things grow stronger. Consider the difference between trees growing in a rain forest and trees growing in a desert. Because water is so plentiful in a rain forest, trees do not need to send their roots very deep. Consequently, even moderate winds can topple a tree in a rain forest.

Effective parenting is a balancing act. It's not good to rescue teens too quickly when stress arises.

But to survive in a desert, trees must send their roots very deep in search of water, enabling them to withstand even very strong winds. Of course, if a tree goes too long without water in a desert, it will wither.

Teens can also benefit from limited amounts of stress. Too much stress can certainly cause problems, but the absence of stress can leave a teen feeling incompetent to handle the challenges of life. Effective parenting requires that parents refrain from "rescuing" their teens too quickly whenever stress arises, while at the same time helping out when their teens experiences too much stress.

Parents can do this by listening to their teens when they are stressed, exploring with them their options for overcoming the stressor, and expressing confidence that their teens can handle the challenge. If, however, your teen starts to experience disruptions in their daily activities, such as difficulty sleeping or eating, this is a strong indication that your teen is being overwhelmed by stress. If so, you should step in to help out.

almost 40 percent of adolescent deaths. That's why insurance companies charge such high rates for teenagers, especially for teenage boys. What's more, when motor vehicle accidents involve a fatality and a teenager is driving, about 50 percent of the time that teenage driver has a blood alcohol level of 0.1 or higher, well above the legal limit in most states.

Unfortunately, too many parents think that adolescence is a time to relax family rules. Nothing could be further from the truth. Indeed, it is especially important that parents of teenagers set and enforce clear limits. This is because the mistakes made during adolescence can have far more drastic and long-lasting consequences than the mistakes made during early childhood. So far from loosening the reins,

the new monitoring challenge: the internet

the Internet represents a new challenge to parents of teenagers. While it can be a wonderful tool for communicating and information gathering, it also contains many dangers for teens, including easily accessible pornographic sites and adult child molesters masquerading as friendly peers. Here are some tips for protecting your teens while at the same time they utilize the benefits of the Internet:

Make learning how to navigate the Internet a family experience. This will give you an opportunity to ensure your teenager understands the rules of Internet use. This also allows you to set a good example for your teen. If, on the other hand, teenagers see their parents accessing "adult" sites or using foul language in chat rooms, they come to see that as appropriate Internet behavior.

Place the computer in a family living area, not in your teenager's bedroom. Having to use

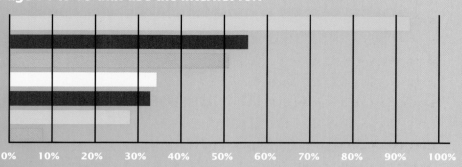

Percentage of youths age 14 to 18 that use the Internet for:

- Finding information
- Surveying music or videos
- Participating in chat rooms
- Making new friends
- Playing video games
- Maintaining relationships
- Buying products

0%   10%   20%   30%   40%   50%   60%   70%   80%   90%   100%

Source: Bama Research Group

a computer in a public area will help reduce the likelihood your teen will explore sites he or she knows are inappropriate or in violation of family rules.

Limit the times that your teenager can be on the Internet. If your teenager is up at 3 in the morning exploring the Internet, he or she may be more inclined to experiment with accessing inappropriate sites. The later the hour, the more likely it is that dangerous adults will be attempting to contact unsuspecting teens and younger children.

parents of teenagers must become increasingly vigilant—precisely because teens are so prone to engaging in high-risk behaviors.

This doesn't mean that teenagers should be denied all opportunities for autonomy and independence. But rather than simply giving them these opportunities by virtue of age alone, teenagers should be required to earn them. Teenagers will, of course, protest this idea, but deep down even they know that they are not yet ready to be on their own.

The good news is parents are the most influential factor in the decision of teenagers to engage in high-risk behaviors. Research consistently finds that warm, accepting, and authoritative parenting during the teenage years is associated with

Do not allow your teen to participate in unsupervised chat rooms. Here's where real danger lies. Anyone can log onto a chat room and disguise their true identity and purpose. Even monitored and supervised chat rooms can pose dangers. This is one way that predators can acquire a teenager's e-mail address. It is best, therefore, to allow your teenager to participate in chats only with people they already know.

Use search engines that filter out adult and other inappropriate Web sites. Unfiltered search engines can result in a teenager innocently stumbling upon a pornographic or hate-inspired Web site. Often these sites will use innocent sounding search words, like "doll" or even "puppies," to direct traffic to their websites. Make sure your teenagers only have access to search engines that filter out this kind of garbage. Some, like SearchHound and Lycos SafteyNet, provide filters that only allow access to sites appropriate for kids. Yahoo!, one of the most popular search engines, now provides a youth version called Yahooligans!

Trust, but verify. Every once in a while, you should check the files that have been downloaded by your computer's Internet browser. Some software programs, like Net Nanny, provide detailed reports of the sites your computer has visited. Let your teenager know in advance you are going to do this, which will help them resist the temptation to go where they know they ought not go.

Don't allow your teenager to become an Internet addict. The Internet can be a valuable tool. It should not become a lifestyle. Limit the overall amount of time your teenager (and you) spend on the Internet on a daily or weekly basis. Encourage your teen to engage in old-fashioned activities, like reading and sports, that don't require a computer.

Have a good relationship with your teen. In the end, the most important protection you have against the dangers of the Internet is not a filtered search engine, but a good and open relationship with your teen.

Stay informed. It's a good idea to keep up with what's happening on the Internet and on ways to protect your teens. To the right are some good books that can help you get started.

Safety Net: Guiding and Guarding Your Children on the Internet
by Zachary Britton
Harvest House, 1998

Silicon Snake Oil: Second Thoughts on the Information Superhighway
by Clifford Stoll
Doubleday, 1995

Protecting Children in Cyberspace
by Stephen J. Kavanagh
Behavioral Psychotherapy Center, 1997

teens' greater self-restraint from high-risk behaviors. Having a good relationship with your teen is not enough. You also have to monitor him or her closely.

Watching Your Teens

Parents who know where their kids are and supervise their activities are the least likely to have teens who smoke, drink, have sex, or get into trouble with the law. It is important to keep in mind that parental awareness of high-risk behavior is not the same thing as parental monitoring. Nor is mere awareness sufficient to protect adolescents from engaging in high-risk behaviors.

Research, for example, has shown that parents who are aware their teens drink alcohol tend to have teens who are more, not less, likely to drink and drive. The lesson: Simply increasing your knowledge of your teen's whereabouts and activities will not reduce deviant behaviors. This awareness must be accompanied by effective parenting practices to reduce deviant behaviors or foster more appropriate, prosocial behavior. For details on these practices, see "Parenting Teens," on page 48.

Not only do positive parenting practices and good family relationships contribute to greater self-restraint in the teenage years, they also have positive effects that last well into adulthood.

According to research conducted by Lawrence Fisher, Ph.D., professor at the School of Medicine, University of California at San Francisco, and and S. Shirley Feldman, Ph.D., associate director of the Program in Human Biology at Stanford University in California, adolescents who perceive their families as emotionally close, orderly, and stable (compared to those reared in emotionally disconnected families) engage in significantly fewer risky behaviors. These teens are less likely to regularly drink alone, drive a car while under the influence of alcohol, engage in promiscuous sexual activity, use drugs, or smoke cigarettes.

In fact, this research shows that family emotional closeness during adolescence is a more powerful predictor of whether teens would engage in high-risk behaviors than is the youth's own personal and emotional functioning, including self-esteem and overall mental health. In other words, teens who feel close to their families are less likely to put themselves in danger.

Given that good parental practices and family relations reduce the probability of high-risk behavior, it is not surprising that ineffective parenting and poor family relations increase the odds that a teenager will engage in high-risk behavior. In fact, parental conflict and inconsistency, the absence of parental monitoring, coercive parent-teen relationships, and parental drug and alcohol

Tips for Handling High-Risk Behavior:

Be a part of your teen's life. Before and after school, at dinner, and before bed are key times.

Be approachable. Let your teen know you two can talk openly anytime.

Be crystal clear. Send clear messages about what constitutes acceptable behavior.

Keep harmful substances out of the house. These include cigarettes, drugs, and alcohol. Teens with access to these are more likely to use them.

Have high expectations. Teens who sense their parents' expectations report less emotional distress.

Help your teen become involved in school activities. Higher attachment to school activities also lowers risk behaviors.

Source: The National Longitudinal Study of Adolescent Health/Add Health

younger and older teens

adolescence is not an event, it is an ongoing process. Young adolescents (the years from about 12 until about a year after puberty) are as different from older adolescents (the ensuing period up until college age) as the infant is from the kindergartner. Here are some key differences:

Young Adolescents	Older Adolescents
Want more independence and freedom, but with little sense of responsibility for the consequences of their actions	Increasingly likely to accept responsiblity for the consequences of their own actions
Are extremely concerned with fitting in with their peers; focused on popularity	Still interested in peers, but with more focus on close friendships rather than mere popularity
Often fumbling in relations toward the opposite sex; seek out information from books, TV, and films	Pair off more frequently with members of the opposite sex; are more confident in their knowledge about sex
Conflicts with parents increase as they seek more time with peers	Conflicts with parents begin to decline as teen approaches late adolescence
Display greater intimacy toward parents; still spend a lot of time with family	Report less intimacy with parents and spend less time with them
Begin to experiment with personal religious and moral beliefs	Personal religious and moral beliefs are more well solidified
Are concerned with who they are and how they fit into the world	Are more concerned with what they are going to do with their lives

And teens of all ages, including older adolescents, see their parents as their primary sources of support and advice regarding such important aspects of their lives as school, friends, and future employment. Of course, every teenager is an individual and there can be exceptions to the above.

use are all linked to high-risk behaviors during adolescence. What all this means is that you as a parent have a pretty important role to play.

Other Risk Factors

Running around in a deviant peer group can lead to risky behavior. Although parents have the most influence on whether or not teens decide to engage in high-risk behaviors in the first place, it turns out that peers have a greater influence on whether or not the teen will continue to engage in high-risk behavior.

Lest you think that only parents and peers influence a teen's decision to engage in high risk-behaviors, there is one more factor: the teenager himself or herself, and especially the teen's temperament. Research has shown that a number of things contribute to high-risk behaviors in adolescents:

Depression

Poor impulse control

An inability to assess risk accurately

Low self-esteem

In addition, teens with highly active and sensation-seeking temperaments have difficulty following rules when no one is watching, use alcohol and drugs earlier and more frequently, express less empathy, and provide selfish and antisocial solutions to moral dilemmas.

In summary, three things contribute to your teen's decision to engage in or not to engage in high-risk behaviors:

• You

• Your teen's peers

• Your teen himself or herself

It doesn't take a Ph.D. to figure out that only one of these things is under your control—you. You can serve either as a protective factor for your teen or as an additional stressor that can disrupt your teen's adjustment. Most of the time, if you play your cards right, you can be the deciding influence for good.

Why Peers Are So Darned Important

Peers become increasingly important during the teenage years. Peers are especially influential about such things as dress and appearance, leisure-time activities, and language. Most of the time, peer relationships during the teenage years are a good thing. Peer relationships help teenagers develop the social skills necessary for adult functioning, are instrumental in facilitating an adolescent's sense of personal identity, and aid in their efforts to achieve independence and autonomy from their family.

Unfortunately, peers also have a downside. In addition to the good stuff, peers can also provide a negative role model for deviant behavior, encourage inappropriate risk taking, and cause intense feelings of inadequacy and depression when they tease, bully, or are otherwise rejecting.

These are two major factors to keep in mind when considering teenagers and the importance of their peer relationships: popularity and close friendships.

Desperately Seeking Popularity

Everybody wants to be popular with their peers. Only the most cold-hearted curmudgeon among us doesn't care what others think. But with teenagers, peer

The Bewitching Hours Contrary to what many parents think, the most likely time for teens to get into trouble is not the evening or weekends. Rather, the most high-risk time is between the hours of 3 and 6 p.m.—after school lets out and before parents get home from work.

According to the National Campaign to Prevent Teen Pregnancy, this is the most likely time for teens to engage in sex. It is also a peak time for juvenile crime. Another high-risk time is summer vacation.

If there is not a parent at home when school lets out or during summer vacations, parents should take care to ensure their teens are adequately supervised. Some ways to do this are:

Find appropriate activities. Enroll them in supervised activities when a parent is not home.

group acceptance and popularity become an obsession. What are other teenagers wearing? What would my friends think? Would the other kids think this behavior/clothing style/way of talking/choice in music is cool? These are the questions most teens ask themselves about every 5 seconds or so.

This desire to be accepted by one's peers means that one of the worst things that can befall teenagers is to be embarrassed in front of their friends. It's the

> For your teenager to develop effective conflict-resolution skills, you will have to resist the urge to jump in and rescue your teen too quickly when he or she is in the midst of a fight with a friend.

reason teenagers see every pimple as if it the were size of a walnut, can't walk past a mirror or reflecting window without checking themselves out, follow the latest fashions with the intensity of a laser beam, and insist their parents refrain from any display of public affection. If you keep in mind that the "prime directive" of teenagers is to avoid being embarrassed in front of their peers, you will avoid a lot of problems with your teen.

Friends Count

But popularity is not the only thing when it comes to teenagers and their peers. In fact, it's not even the most important factor. Far more important than popularity is whether or not a teen has at least one close friendship.

Close friendships during the teenage years serve several important functions. They provide companionship, emotional support, nonsexualized intimacy, and a means of expressing emotions and resolving conflicts. The real danger sign that something is wrong is not that your teen is not elected to be class president, but if he or she does not have at least one close friendship.

This doesn't mean your teen's friendships always have to be smooth and non-combative. Teens do get into arguments and fights with even their close friends. Learning how to resolve peer conflicts is an important part of adolescence. In these situations you can lend a sympathetic ear and offer occasional advice—but only occasional.

◀ **Expect a call.** Require that they call in when they get home from school.

Think about employment and enjoyment. During summer vacations, either require that your teen work in a supervised setting (provided he or she is of sufficient age), or enroll him or her in a summer camp or activity for teens.

Set firm rules. Let your teens know exactly what is acceptable and not acceptable in your absence. Hint: having opposite-sex friends over the house in your absence should never be acceptable.

Check it out. Occasionally, go home early from work for a surprise "inspection." Do this to verify that your teen is following the rules you've agreed upon. Let your teen know you will do this from time to time, but don't tell your teen when or how frequently you might do this.

For your teenager to develop effective conflict-resolution skills, you will have to resist the urge to jump in and rescue your teen too quickly when he or she is in the midst of a fight with a friend.

Developing Social Skills

Two things can get in the way of your teen developing good peer relationships:
- A lack of appropriate social skills
- Fear of rejection by peers

Ideally, good peer social skills begin developing way back in the preschool years (remember those sandbox fights?), continue to develop during elementary school,

Ideally, good peer social skills begin developing way back in the preschool years ... and become more refined during adolescence.

and become more refined during adolescence. Skills such as active listening, taking turns, playing fair, perspective taking, and sharing are all necessary for good peer relationships, not just in adolescence, but in adulthood as well.

If your teen is having problems making and maintaining friendships, there are

teenagers: a recent invention

I t may come as a surprise to learn that the age we call "adolescence" is a relatively recent phenomenon. Up until about 100 years ago, and in many primitive societies even today, there was no concept of adolescence. Rather, rituals called puberty rites or rites of passage—often carefully timed to coincide with puberty—ushered young people from the world of childhood directly into the world of adulthood.

Sometimes these initiation rites into adulthood were relatively simple, such as a change of clothing or hairstyles. Other initiation rituals were more complex, even bizarre by today's standards, involving such things as

Primitive initiation rituals were more complex, even bizarre by today's standards.

having one's teeth filed to a point, elaborate tattooing, periods of fasting or isolation, engaging in mortal combat, circumcision with a sharp stick, or surgical removal of the clitoris. As bizarre or elaborate as these initiation rituals might have been, rarely did they last longer than a few weeks. As societies became more complex and industrialized, there came a need for greater preparation to take on adult roles. Industrialized nations now require about seven years for the transition from childhood to adulthood. That period gets filled with things like learning to drive and attending high school and, increasingly, college.

Still, remnants of an earlier age when rites of passage were conducted with much younger children remain with us today. Both the Christian tradition of confirmation, when an individual is asked to confirm his or her own religious belief, and the Jewish traditional Bar and Bat Mitzvahs, occur at about age 13.

So the next time your teen asks how come you don't treat him or her like an adult, perhaps you might want to relay to your teen that historically many societies did treat 13- and 14-year-olds as adults. Only thing is, to prove they were adults, they might have had to have their teeth sharpened into points.

some structured, behaviorally oriented social skills training programs for adolescents that can help. You can get information about these programs from either guidance counselors at your teen's school or a mental health professional. The best teacher is a good example. So if you want your teen to display effective social skills, be sure to display them yourself.

Just as debilitating as a lack of social skills, and sometimes even more so, is social anxiety. Social anxiety refers to an overwhelming fear that other teens will not accept you. This anxiety both inhibits social interaction and leads directly to social problems for teens. The perception of social exclusion from one's peer group often contributes to feelings of anxiety, which in turn limits peer interactions. Girls seem to be especially vulnerable to high levels of social anxiety and especially to fears of negative peer evaluations. Research confirms that girls are more concerned about others' judgments of their appearance and behavior, and, as a result, rates of depression and anxiety are higher among teenage girls than among teenage boys. This tendency to be more vulnerable to social anxiety even carries over into adulthood, where adult women are about twice as likely to experience anxiety in social situations as men.

While you may be tempted to enjoy your teenager's withdrawal from other teenagers (and their negative influence), social anxiety in the teenage years is a problem that needs attention. Two things are pretty good predictors of whether or not a youngster will experience depression during the teen years—the quality of friendships and whether or not a teen is popular. This is especially so for girls.

If socially anxious teens perceive their general social acceptance or romantic appeal to be low, this may lead them to miss out on important socialization experiences and, over time, may contribute to impairments in adult social functioning. Indeed, studies with adults have shown those with social phobias are less likely to marry than those who are comfortable in social situations.

The Dating Game

Although an increased interest in the opposite sex is a natural and normal part of adolescence, don't be fooled into believing that sexual relations between teens is as well. Despite all the popular media accounts of rampant sex among teenagers, teen sex is neither inevitable nor desirable.

Tips for Monitoring Teens

Keep an eye on your teenagers. You don't need to be a spy. But you do need to monitor their behavior. Why? Researchers have found that poor parental monitoring is one of the most potent predictors of adolescent involvement in virtually any problem behavior. In other words, if you don't watch now ... you will have to watch out for what follows!

Indeed, the evidence suggests that parents endanger their teens' development when they abdicate their responsibility to attend to and participate in the lives of their kids.

Here are some tips for effectively monitoring your teens:

- Become familiar with their entertainment. Find out what they like to watch and listen to, and try to understand why.

- Set a family standard. Be clear about what's acceptable and what's not.

- Set an example. Make good entertainment choices yourself. Apologize to your teenager if you find yourself engaging in hypocritical behavior.

- Get to know your teenager's friends—by name. This will impress your teenager while at the same time assuring your teen that you are keeping a watchful eye over their peer relationships and activities.

One of your jobs as parent is to communicate clearly and unequivocally that you think teenagers having sex is wrong. If you do, your teen will be much less likely to engage in sexual activity than if you give a fuzzier "I'm not going to tell you what to do" message.

According to the National Longitudinal Study of Adolescent Risk Behavior, the largest study of its kind ever undertaken, youth who perceive their parents as giving them a clear message that abstinence from sex is the expected behavior during adolescence were the most likely to delay the onset of sexual activity and avoid becoming pregnant as a teenager.

Another way to help your teen avoid having sex while an adolescent is to discourage early dating. According to the National Campaign to Prevent Teen Pregnancy, dating should be discouraged, if not prohibited, until your teen is 16 years old, and even then dating should occur in groups and in venues that are well supervised. Unless, that is, you have an overwhelming desire to be called "Grandma" or "Grandpa" real soon.

Take your teens' peer relationships and anxieties seriously. Peer relationships are important for developing a host of positive qualities in your teen. At the same time, don't surrender your teen to his or her peers. Deviant peer groups can cause all sorts of difficulties.

In fact, research shows that the more time teenagers spend interacting with their parents, the less likely they are to be influenced by peers—at least on the big stuff, like using drugs, drinking, driving recklessly, and having sex.

If you want your teen's behavior to reflect your values and beliefs, make sure

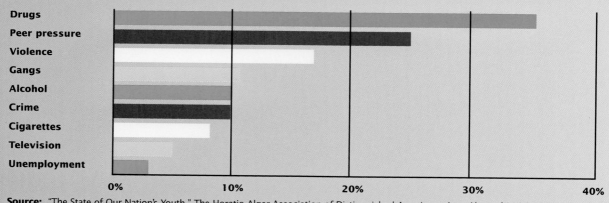

Percentage of youths age 14 to 18 that rate the worst influences on teens as:

Source: "The State of Our Nation's Youth," The Horatio Alger Association of Distinguished Americans, Inc., Alexandria, VA 1997.

you spend time with your teen. Living with a teenager may at times be difficult, but being a teenager is even harder.

Their task is to achieve a healthy sense of self-identity while avoiding the pitfalls of high-risk adolescent behavior. Doing so requires good peer relationships, but also avoiding deviant peer groups. It also means exploring the world of romantic interests while avoiding the world of teenage parenthood.

Adolescence is the journey your children must go through in order to get to adulthood. To get there, teens must traverse a great deal of uncharted, and often turbulent, territory. You can't make that journey for them. But you can offer shelter when it storms.

The Lucky Ones

Not all teenagers and their parents experience tension and conflict. Some teens and their parents experience almost no conflict at all, except for the inevitable frictions that go along with living together. Such families manage to let go of their

While encouraging your teen to spend time with peers is a good thing, if you want your teen's behavior to reflect your values and beliefs, make sure you spend time with your teen as well.

teens easily and confidently, and remain emotionally close even after physical separation.

Three things contribute to such nonconflict families:

- An easygoing temperament style
- An early identification with the family's values, beliefs, and traditions
- The teen being a girl

Of course, the more typical situation is one in which there is a certain amount of "storm and stress" as the teen grows increasingly independent from the family and the family learns to let go.

So if you are one of these rare exceptions, lucky enough to have a teen that presents almost no conflict, here's a prediction: Bragging about it to other parents of teens will not win you any friends.

4

parenting teens

Someone once quipped, "The trouble with kittens is that, sooner or later, they become cats."

as some would have it, so it is with babies. Sooner or later, they become teenagers. Yikes!

But this is too harsh a view. The truth is parents can—and most do—have a good relationship with their teenagers. Just ask their teenagers. By large majorities, teenagers say their parents have a good understanding of what they want to do in life, know what is happening to them in school, and are relatively easy to talk to about things that interest or trouble them.

According to one recent survey of 12- to 17-year-olds, 81 percent agreed that "I can always trust my parents to be there for me when I need them," whereas only 62 percent said the same thing about friends.

In fact, more than 82 percent of teens ages 14 to 18 report they have little or no difficulty getting along with their mothers. And 79 percent say the same thing about their fathers. Way to go, Mom and Dad!

Teens also respect the fact that their parents, and not they, should be the ultimate arbiters for such things as getting married, staying out late, using birth control, and driving a car. Most are less willing, however, to abdicate to parents decisions about body piercing or dying their hair.

Your job is to guide your teen through some of the most difficult years of his or her life while giving increasing amounts of responsibility.

So the good news is that teen-parent relationships are frequently not as troubled as is commonly thought.

Teens Want Closer Ties

Teens typically like their parents, believe their parents know what is happening in their lives, are confident that their parents will be there for them when they need them, and also respect their parents' authority.

But there is also some bad news. Family time, while certainly not vanishing, is diminishing. Most parents today wish they could spend more time together as a family. And so do their teens. According to one nationwide survey, 68 percent of teens wish they could spend more time with their fathers and 64 percent wish they could spend more time with their mothers.

Perhaps the saddest commentary of all is this: Nearly one in five sixth through twelfth graders say they have not had a single good conversation lasting at least 10 minutes with a parent in the past month. At the very time our children need us the most—when they are teens—one in five hasn't had a single good conversation with one of their parents in over a month.

One consequence of diminishing family time is that parents—the single most influential factor in a teenager's life—are increasingly less likely to be around to exert that influence. Without the steadying hand and watchful eyes of an involved parent, teens can, and do, get into all sorts of difficulties.

Despite ever-increasing material affluence, the fact is on most measures of child well-being—including alcohol and illicit drug use, cigarette smoking, and teen pregnancy—teenagers today are doing worse than teenagers just two or three generations ago.

Herein lies the awesome responsibility of parenting teenagers. Your job is to guide your teenager through some of the most difficult and potentially dangerous years of his or her life while giving your teen increasing amounts of responsibility and autonomy. Life doesn't get any more challenging than this.

Home Sweet Home

Contrary to popular perception, most teens report having a good relationship with their parents:

82% rate their parents' understanding of what their teens want to do in life as either excellent or good.

75% say their parents usually know what's happening in school.

75% say at home they often talk with adults about things that interest them or are troubling them.

71% say their family eats at least one meal together each day.

69% say they enjoy family mealtime.

68% say after school there is usually an adult at home.

67% rate their parents' understanding of the problems they face growing up as excellent or good.

61% rate their parents' understanding of the peer pressures they face as excellent or good.

55% say on weekends their family does a lot of things together.

Source: Nationwide survey of teenagers 13 to 17 years old by Gallup, November 1996 to June 1997.

Three General Rules

Everyone without a teenager in the house is an expert; everyone with a teenager in the house is at least a little bit confused. Fortunately, we do know something about effectively parenting teenagers and it is this: Effective parenting requires love, limits, and consistency.

Rule 1: Love and Warmth

The first ingredient for effective parenting is being warm and affectionate. Whereas high degrees of parental warmth are associated with self-confident children with high self-esteem, parental hostility is associated with aggressive children and especially with juvenile delinquency.

Parental warmth is important because it enhances a teen's desire to be like his or her parents and to follow and internalize parental rules. Parents who are warm and affectionate are also better able to use withdrawal of affection as a disciplinary technique instead of harsher, more physical discipline.

Love and warmth are the foundation upon which all other parenting practices rests. For everything else to work—communication, problem solving, consistency, and limit setting—parents need to make their teens feel wanted and needed. Nothing else works if teens believe their parents do not really love them, go out of their way to hurt their feelings, or ignore them as long as they do not bother them.

Here are a few things to keep in mind.

Don't let yourself get bent out of shape. Let's face it. It's hard to be warm and loving when your teen is being disrespectful, screaming at you at the top of his or

Declining Family Time

Many parents today report having less family time than they remember having when they were growing up.

Event	Today	When parents grew up
Family usually eats dinner together	80%	92%
Family usually attends religious services together	59%	72%
Parent usually there when child gets home from school	61%	78%
Parent usually attends child's events like school plays and sporting events	94%	79%

Source: Survey of mothers with children under the age of 18 by the Pew Research Center for the People & the Press, March 14 to 26, 1997.

her lungs for setting a limit, or taking for granted what you do as favors, like that 20th trip to the mall this week. Sometimes teens even define themselves, at least temporarily, by how different they can be from their parents. When they do, it's awfully hard not to feel rejected.

Apologize when you lose it. Remember, you are the adult. You must draw upon your greater maturity to ensure that you do not say hurtful things in response to your teen's provocations. And if you do (and all parents do once in a while), it's important to apologize.

Discipline as needed. Loving your teen doesn't mean never disciplining him or her. In fact, effective parenting requires that you sometimes discipline your teenager. But discipline should come out of love, not because you are angry, frustrated, or upset. This is especially so (and tricky) during the teenage years when your teen's behavior can provoke such intense feelings.

Keep the focus on behavior. One way to help ensure your teenager does not misinterpret discipline as rejection is to separate out the behavior you dislike

Another good guide to setting effective limits with teenagers is to avoid creating overly dramatic consequences for ordinary misbehavior.

from the teenager you love. Instead of saying, "Look at this room! What a mess! You are the biggest slob that ever lived!," say (calmly, if possible), "You need to clean up your room before you go out." Instead of saying, "After all I've done for you, how dare you talk to me that way! You're such a brat!," say, "I don't like it when you show disrespect to me."

Express your loving feelings. Another way to help assure your teen of your ongoing love, no matter what, is to look for those moments—every day—when you can express affection toward your teen. Saying "I love you" and giving frequent hugs can go a long way toward communicating to teens how much you care for them.

Strive for five. If you're having some trouble with all this, challenge yourself to say something nice to your teen five times a day to help you get back into the habit. Just don't expect that your teen will always reciprocate. And when he or she doesn't, resist the urge to feel rejected. Just have confidence that underneath that scowling exterior, your expressions of love and affection are having an impact.

Rule 2: Setting Limits

Love is not enough. Parents need to combine high warmth with moderate degrees of control and restrictiveness. We're not talking about being a cold, distant martinet, barking out orders and demanding swift compliance and a firm "Yes, sir!" (Although that would be nice once in a while, wouldn't it?) Indeed, too much parental control, especially if there is an absence of affection, is associated with teens that act out their emotions and frustrations in negative ways.

Rather, what we are talking about is parents being ready, willing, and able to set clear limits with certain consequences when those limits are breached. Instead of giving some vague command like, "Get home at a reasonable hour or you're going to be in big trouble!," say (again, as calmly as possible), "Your curfew is eleven. If you are not home by then, you will not be able to go out for the rest of the weekend."

Try "Grandma's Rule." This is a good guide for setting limits with teenagers. Essentially Grandma's Rule is this: First you do what I want you to do, and then you get to do what you want to do. Some examples might be, "First you must clean your room, and then you can watch TV," or "First you must do your homework, and then you can talk on the phone." You motivate your teen to do what you want by making a bargain. They get to do something they want after complying with your request.

Never give in. The key to using Grandma's Rule is to make sure that both what you want to happen and what your teen wants to do are clearly stated in advance. After giving this kind of instruction, don't nag, cajole, or badger them. Doing so will only invite conflict and arguments about the "fairness" of the rule. And who needs more arguments? Instead, simply enforce the rule with as much calmness as you can muster. (There's that darn "calm" word again!) And never, never give in—unless you actually enjoy being pestered by your teen.

Grandma's rule works so well that psychologists have given it a fancy name. They call it the Premack Principle. The idea is that humans can be motivated to engage in a less desired behavior if they are then allowed to do a more desired behavior afterwards. But grandmas were doing this long before there were psychologists around. Psychologists just like to give fancy names to things that just come naturally to grandmas.

Let the punishment fit the crime. Another good guide to setting effective limits with teenagers is to avoid creating overly dramatic consequences for ordinary misbehavior. Don't say, "If you come home even five minutes late, you will be grounded for a month!" First of all, the punishment really doesn't fit the crime. Coming home five minutes late is not the worst sin in the world. And inevitably, you'll give in anyway and won't enforce the punishment.

It's much better to give small punishments consistently than large punishments inconsistently. In this example, you might say instead, "You came home five minutes after curfew, and so tomorrow night's curfew will be thirty minutes earlier than usual."

Be firm. Your teenager will, of course, whine and complain about your setting limits. Your teenager may even say you're the meanest, rottenest parent in the whole wide world and that you are making life miserable by setting a limit or imposing a negative consequence for violating a household rule. Don't you believe it, not even for a second. Research consistently shows that parents who set and enforce reasonable limits rear teenagers with higher self-esteem, adaptability, competence, internalized control, and popularity with peers.

In fact, while no teenager will ever actually admit this (to do so would violate the secret code of teenagerhood), teens actually want their parents to set limits on their behavior. Remember that the primary task of the teen years is to determine just how independent and autonomous they can be from their parents and family. This requires testing the limits of their ability to be independent. But underneath they are unsure as to how independent and autonomous they can be. So they quietly hope that their parents will rein them in if they start to get themselves into trouble. If their parents don't do this, teens either get a false sense of their own competence or, even worse, think their parents don't care about them.

So when your teen fights with you about nightly curfews, your teen doesn't really want you to say, "Gee, you decide when you want to come home. Any time is OK with me. Stay out all night if you want to!" Being too permissive with teens leaves them feeling adrift in rough and potentially dangerous seas. Despite any protests to the contrary, your teen is counting on you to set them straight when they are headed for trouble.

Explain your rules. It is also a good idea to combine limit setting with explanations for rules and punishments. Explanations help kids of all ages to understand the rules and to internalize them.

This doesn't mean you should lecture your teens; they absolutely hate that. What it does mean is that when you establish a rule or set a limit, you should combine it with an explanation for why you are doing so. A simple and calm (there's that word again!) statement such as, "Your curfew is eleven on school days because you need enough sleep to do well at school" is sufficient.

Don't get physical. One last thing. Teenagers should never be hit. The evidence is quite clear that using corporal punishment, such as spanking, with teenagers always makes things worse. So if you used corporal punishment with your child when he or she was younger, it's time to stop. If you didn't, don't start.

Rule 3: Consistency

Effective parents also need to be consistent. Whether you are tired, frustrated at work, or angry with your spouse, you still have to demonstrate your love for your teen and set firm and consistent limits.

Consistency really is critical. When parents are inconsistent, their teenagers are more likely to engage in aggressive or delinquent behavior. The association between parental inconsistency and aggressive behavior in children is especially strong for boys. In fact, the highest rates of delinquency are found in homes in which both parents are inconsistent in setting and enforcing limits.

The Importance of Good Influences

As important as parents are to teenagers, it is also important that teens are exposed to other caring adults in their community. Encourage your teenager's involvement in activities with grandparents, youth leaders, teachers, and religious leaders who provide sustained guidance, encouragement, and support. This is an important way to help minimize the chances that your teen will be seduced into high-risk and deviant activities. This is especially so for teens whose parents are absent or when families are experiencing a lot of conflict.

It is also helpful to encourage your teenager to become involved in community activities. Experiences that require teenagers to assist others in their neighborhood helps in the development of empathy, responsibility, and other positive social behaviors that help in the transition to productive adulthood.

It may be especially important to encourage your teenager to become involved in faith-based activities. Such involvement aids in the development of a positive moral code of conduct, and makes them less likely to engage in high-risk or deviant activities.

Back your spouse. Being consistent doesn't mean that you and your spouse have to do everything exactly the same. Not only is it impossible for moms and dads to do everything exactly the same, it would make for an awfully boring household if they did. But parents do have to agree on family rules and be willing to back each other up when the rules are breached.

Present a united front. One simple way to do this is the "first in, wins" rule. This means that the first parent to identify a rule infringement and to dish out the

The evidence is quite clear that using corporal punishment, such as spanking, with teenagers always makes things worse.

punishment controls the situation. The role of the other parent is to back the spouse up. There will be plenty of time later—in private—to discuss any disagreements about how the situation was handled. But children—and teenagers especially—need to see a united parental front. When it comes to disciplining teenagers, you need an ally. Hint: That ally is not your teenager.

Teenagers and Rules

Violating any of the three rules is begging for trouble. Parents who are low on warmth, but high on control, tend to have conflicted, irritable, and passively hostile teens frequently lacking in empathy for others. On the other hand, parents who display moderate warmth, but low control, tend to have children who are impulsive and openly aggressive toward others. In contrast, parents who follow these three rules rear teens who are energetic, friendly, cooperative, and helpful. There are exceptions, of course, but these are the rules.

Parental Characteristics and Child Outcomes

If you're one that find charts and graphs helpful, here is an illustration of what happens when teenagers are reared with different types of parenting styles. If you find charts and graphs confusing, just nod knowingly and move on.

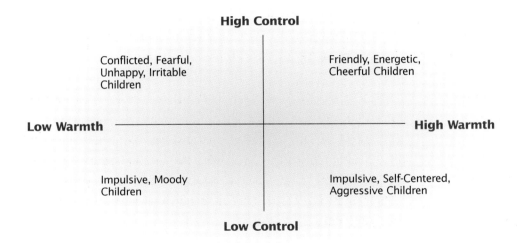

Sounds easy so far, doesn't it? Love your kids, set (and enforce) limits, and be consistent. No problem. But here's the kicker. Whereas applying these three rules to younger children is relatively straightforward, applying them to teenagers is a bit more complicated for two reasons. First, little kids focus on their parents like laser beams. Teens have broadened their focus to include peers, neighborhood standards, and the broader popular culture (which, you've surely noticed, is none too hot when it comes to helping you raise teens). Second, teenagers need to be allowed much more independence and autonomy in decision making than younger children.

Because the world of the adolescent has expanded so dramatically, the teen years can be an extremely confusing time. Behaviors and beliefs taught in and valued by the family often conflict with those valued by peers, the media, and the broader culture. The result can be great inner tension as the adolescent struggles to reconcile these conflicts and settle on a set of personal moral values and principles for living. Essentially, the teen must answer the following question: To whose values will I be loyal? My family's? My peers'? My favorite rock star's?

Ensuring that teens will not overidentify with peers and the popular culture and discard all you have tried to teach them since infancy is, to a very large extent, a matter of your time. Parents who spend time with their teens, doing things of mutual interest, consistently eating meals as a family, and going places together, are in a much better position than those who don't to counter the oftentimes corrupting influence of our modern culture.

Just don't rely on that ridiculous idea of "quality time" to get this done for you. Yes, the time you spend with your teen should be of good quality. But time with your teen is like oxygen. The quality of the oxygen we breath is important, but we also need it in sufficient quantity. High-quality oxygen is not much help if we only get it once or twice a month. The same is true of time.

The more involved parents are in the lives of their teens, the more likely their teens will reflect their parents' values and beliefs rather than those of peers or the popular culture. So if you want your teen to live your values and beliefs, rather than those of that rock star with full body tattoos, navel rings, and songs about the wonders of sex, drugs, and devil worship, you have to be there.

Allowing for Independence

The second factor that makes parenting teens more difficult than parenting younger children is that teenagers need to be given progressively more independence and autonomy in decision making. But when should parents allow teenagers to make their own decisions, and when should they step in and make decisions for them? Good question.

Experts often advise parents to allow their adolescents opportunities to

Tips for Spending Time with Teens:

You've heard that it's important to spend time with your teenager. But what to do? Here are a few suggestions.

- Develop a common interest or hobby.
- Eat meals together.
- Turn off the TV.
- Talk.
- Make your house a peer-friendly place to be.
- Go on family vacations doing things your kids like to do (perhaps allowing them to bring a friend along).
- Work together on a project.
- Play games together.
- Involve your kids in your work.
- Limit your own newspaper and magazine reading time by skimming the headlines and first couple of paragraphs, rather than reading them from cover to cover.

express themselves. Good advice—to a point. Teens do need opportunities for self-expression, but unbridled freedom to experiment can be very dangerous during adolescence.

Teens need supervision precisely because they are so prone to risk taking and testing of the limits. Only actively involved parents can provide the type of intensive supervision and monitoring they need.

In fact, poor parental monitoring is one of the most potent predictors of adolescent involvement in virtually any problem behavior. The evidence is clear: Parents endanger their teens' development when they abdicate their responsibility to attend to and participate in the lives of their teens. Adolescence is no time to pull back from parental responsibility.

And while parents should set and enforce limits on the behavior of their teenagers, at the same time parents need to increasingly use explanation, discussion, and negotiation as disciplinary techniques.

By transforming the parent-child relationship from one based on unilateral authority to one of interdependence and cooperative negotiation, parents are more likely to have their teens seek their advice. This allows for more parental guidance over their teenager's development. One particularly useful technique for doing this, especially for problem behavior, is called behavioral contracting, which will be dealt with shortly.

Drawing the Line

Parents also need to learn to differentiate normal strides toward independence from dangerous behavior. There are many areas where teens can—and should—be allowed a great deal of leeway. Not absolute leeway, but a reasonable amount. Taste in music might be one example. If your teenager chooses to listen to rap music, for example, we would not advise trying to prohibit this unless the lyrics are offensive.

Of course, this requires that you actually know what the lyrics are. This means listening to what your kids are listening to. If the lyrics are misogynistic, racist, or violent, don't hesitate to step in, with an explanation, of course.

Another example might be clothing and hairstyles. Allowing your teenager a certain amount of freedom to choose clothing and hairstyles is not only fine, but helpful in supporting your teen's search for his or her own identity. But sexually provocative clothing and green hair can lead to trouble with other adults and even peers. You should draw the line when the clothing or hairstyles become outlandish or involve permanent changes in bodily tissue (like tattoos).

The Money Question

Another area to consider in encouraging independence is allowances. Allowances should be made contingent on the completion of weekly chores. Giving children an allowance simply because they exist only communicates the lesson that they are entitled to something for nothing. But once your teen has earned that allowance, you should let it be spent as the teen wishes, so long as it is not on items that are dangerous or restricted to adult use, like cigarettes and alcohol.

"What?" you may ask, "Aren't I supposed to make them save some of their money or give a portion to charity or to church?" While doing so would not be the worst thing a parent could do, it's better to only recommend these options to your teenager.

Remember, your teenagers' task is to start making good, independent decisions. Forcing them to save does not accomplish this. Let them have the experience of wanting something, like a trip to the movies, without being able to fulfill the desire—because the money is already spent.

Of course, when they are broke, you have to refrain from rescuing your teens by handing over money or buying them things they would otherwise be required to spend their own money on. Otherwise, you would be teaching them to be spendthrifts, not to cultivate the virtue of saving.

There are many other areas of potential conflict that also allow for a certain amount of independence and autonomy, like reluctance to join a family outing, a sudden announcement that one has become a vegetarian, and monopolizing the phone. But in all these situations, limits ought to be set.

It's one thing to allow your teen to stay home when you go to a friend's house for a routine dinner invitation. It's quite another to give in to your teen's demand that he or she not visit Grandma and Grandpa on Christmas day or be part of the family summer trip to the beach.

In making these decisions, rely on your common sense. Learn to respect that little voice inside you that says, "I think this isn't something I should allow." Indeed, the consequences for being too permissive can be much, much worse in adolescence than the consequences of being a tad too restrictive.

And when your teenager insists that "all the other parents are letting their kids do it," make a phone call or two. Chances are, other parents are feeling just as uneasy about allowing that particular behavior or activity as you are.

Finally, helping your teen make good decisions means

Communicating with Teenagers

To talk with teenagers, you have to listen. We mean really listen. Not just pretend listening. You have to really want to hear what your teenager has to say.

A good listener is an active listener. A good listener allows the teen to fully express himself or herself before jumping in with another point of view. A good listener may ask questions for clarification but never interrupts. A good listener also rephrases what the teen has just said, before moving on to stating his or her own point of view.

Good listeners use a **LADDER***:

Look at your teenager

Ask clarifying questions

Don't interrupt

Don't change the subject

Empathize with your teen

Respond only after your teen has had his or her say

Here's an important tip: If you practice talking effectively with your teens about the small stuff, like favorite TV shows, musical preferences, and clothing styles, your teen will feel more comfortable talking with you about the big stuff, like sex, drugs, and alcohol.

Finally, a good listener looks for opportunities to listen. When you are riding in the car on those seemingly endless trips to the mall, for example, keep the radio turned off. You may be amazed at what your teen might say when there is silence to fill.

***Source:** *Bits and Pieces*, vol. T/No. 2, p. 12 (Fairfield, NJ: The Economics Press, 1998).

being a model for those good decisions yourself. If you don't want your teen to smoke cigarettes, don't smoke yourself. If you don't want your teen to drink alcohol, don't get sloshed when you come home from work. If you don't want your teen to drive recklessly, don't drive recklessly yourself. The best sermon is a good example.

The point is this. Soon, your teenager will be on his or her own. Over the six or seven years of adolescence teens need practice in independent decision making. You should provide your son or daughter with that practice so long as it does not pose a danger to your teen or to others, or create problems with peers or other adults.

Handling Problem Behavior

Many of the conflicts that parents and teens experience involve relatively minor disagreements over such common issues as dress, hairstyles, chores, and school work. Still, what distinguishes functional from dysfunctional parent-teen relationships isn't the presence of parent-teen conflict. Rather what distinguishes well-functioning from dysfunctional families is whether or not conflict occurs within a context of overall family closeness.

In fact, parent-teen conflict within the context of a supportive parental relationship

Refrain from rescuing your teens by handing over money or buying them things they would otherwise be required to spend their own money on.

can have positive outcomes. These include learning conflict-resolution skills, taking perspective, and a better sense of self.

Teens can tolerate conflict and arguments if they know that their parents love and care about them and are on their side. Parent-teen relationships that are bankrupt of mutual love, respect, and enjoyment provide few incentives for either the parent or the teen to reconcile differences and resolve arguments.

Setting Up a Behavioral Contract

The best way to handle problem behavior is to anticipate it. One way to anticipate problem behavior, and to cope with it effectively, is with a technique known as behavioral contracting. Here's how you do it.

Step One: Tell your teen that you would like to talk to him or her about something. Then ask your teen to give you some times when it would be convenient to talk. Avoid imposing a time on your teen. This will only invite an argument. But don't let your teen get away with saying, "Oh, maybe next year." You have to a use a little common sense.

Step Two: Once both you and your teen agree on a time, conduct the negotiation session in a neutral site, like the family room or kitchen. Don't hold the meeting in your bedroom or home office. Your teen will see this as "your turf" and will make him or her even more defensive. But neither should you hold this meeting on your teen's turf—the teen's bedroom, for example.

Do not include members of the family who have no business being there in this negotiation session. If you're going to talk about curfew with your 15-year-old, for

example, his 8-year-old brother does not need to be a part of that conversation.

Step Three: Begin by clearly describing the problem behavior. Calmly describe for your teenager the behavior about which you are concerned. Tell your teen you think things would be more pleasant around the home if that particular behavior changed. Then ask your teen his or her opinion about the problem and really listen while your teen answers. Sometimes teens are not aware that a certain behavior is a problem. Just making your teen aware of the behavior can help to change it.

Step Four: Explain that you have a plan, called a behavioral contract, that may help solve the problem. Then describe as precisely as possible the more appropriate behavior you want from your teen instead of the problem behavior. You might say, for example, "Instead of staying up late talking on the phone, I want you to be in bed by eleven so that you will have plenty of rest for school." Or, "Instead of teasing your little brother, I would prefer to see the two of you get along better."

Ask your teen if he or she is able to perform the more appropriate behavior you are requesting. Sometimes teens have good reasons why a particular behavior is not possible. Be willing to listen to the other side of the story.

Step Five: Formalize a plan for changing the behavior. Make sure your teenager understands that coming up with this plan is something you want to work on together. Basically, the plan has two parts: The first part is the benefit to your teenager if he or she follows the plan (such as use of the family car, allowance, some cool clothes). The second part is the consequences to your teen if he or she violates the plan (such as no TV, no phone, no car).

You need to negotiate incentives for following the plan, and disincentives for not following the plan. It is important that you put this plan in writing.

Step Six: Monitor the plan. If adjustments are necessary, discuss these with your teen. Do not simply impose changes unilaterally. And make very sure that you comply with the conditions of the plan yourself. This means extending privileges when they are warranted and imposing consequences when they are warranted. Also, where appropriate, make

Effective Versus Ineffective Families:

High Functioning families are characterized by:

- Emotional bondedness/love
- Commonness/mutuality— "we're in this together"
- Good and expressive communication
- Time together
- A spiritual/religious commitment
- Adaptability and flexibility
- Clarity of family rules

Poorly functioning families are characterized by:

- Marital problems
- Negative and harsh discipline
- Parental withdrawal/ disengagement or depression
- Parental anti-social personality disorder, alcoholism, or drug use
- Rejection
- Lack of warmth
- Less paternal supervision

teen temperament

emperament is the personality characteristics with which a child is born. They include things like how emotional we are, how active we like to be, how easily we adapt to change, and how much structure and routine we like or need.

Research has shown that it is not so much a child's temperament that causes problems, but a mismatch between the child's temperament and the parents' way of treating the child. To rear successful teenagers you need to recognize the kind of temperament your teen has and adjust your parenting practices to fit that temperament. Often, these different types of inborn characteristics cluster together to form different personality or temperament types. The three most common, and the best ways to parent children with these temperament styles, are:

Easygoing: These are the kids we all planned on having. They are generally pleasant in mood, get along easily with others, are relatively even (and mild) tempered, react to change with a minimum of discomfort, and establish regular routines. If your teen is one of these, count your lucky stars.

Slow to Warm Up: While generally even tempered and of positive mood, they are very sensitive to change. Their initial reaction to changes in their situation or environment is withdrawal and clamming up. The key to parenting slow-to-warm-up teens is to give them advance warning and preparation when change is on the way and allow them time to adjust.

> **Your job is to determine your teen's basic temperament style and to adjust to it.**

Difficult or Strong Willed: These teens tend to be highly active and sensation seeking, easily distracted, and irregular in mood. They also are more likely to violate rules for conduct when not being supervised, test limits and engage in risk taking, have more difficulty delaying gratification, and express less empathy for others. The keys to parenting the difficult or strong-willed teen are clear rules, lots of parental supervision and

Dad, I was late because my friends were all going out for pizza after the game and I wanted to go along. What's the big deal? Besides, it's only 11:30. It's not like I was out until 3 in the morning. Give me a break!

The point is, you told us you were coming home right after the basketball game. Your mother and I worry about you when you're not home when you promised you would be. Next time call, or no more basketball this month.

monitoring, and patience and consistency. The good news is that many teens with difficult temperaments evidence a radical turnaround when they get into their twenties. So don't give up—better days are ahead!

Not all kids fit neatly into one of these three categories. Some teens show signs of two or even all three categories at different times and under different circumstances. And keep in mind that teens do not pick their temperament. Your job is to determine your teen's basic temperament style and to adjust to it. The best-functioning families are those in which there is a good "fit" between parenting practices and a teen's temperament style.

additional comments to your teenager about how pleased you are with any cooperation with the contract.

Keep It Simple

When you engage in behavioral contracting it is important that you work on only one problem at a time. Trying to accomplish too much, all at once, is a sure pathway to failure. The focus should be on clearly defined behavioral change—one behavior at a time. As James Dobson, author and president of Focus on the Family has stated so well, you, the parent, have the car a teenager needs, the money he or she covets, and the authority to grant or withhold privileges. Use the power.

But at the same time, make sure you invite the active involvement of your teen

managing teenage behavior

f you're going to be successful in managing annoying and troublesome teenager behavior, you're going to need a plan. Here is a sequence of questions you can ask yourself in deciding how to respond:

Question One: Is this behavior something I can live with? Some teenage behavior, while annoying, is relatively minor and largely an expression of the desire for increased autonomy and independence.

Some examples may be taste in music (within reason), spending lots of time on the phone (so long as homework and household chores are being completed), wanting to spend time with peers rather than family (so long as they are not completely closing themselves off from family events), and clothing styles (again, within reason). So long as the behavior does not violate your parental sensibilities and is not dangerous or destructive, your job is to act primarily as an observer. Resist even the urge to comment on it, unless you actually enjoy arguments with your teenager.
Parental response: Hush up.

Question Two: Does this behavior invite a natural negative consequence? Some annoying or troublesome behavior leads to a natural negative consequence. If so, be grateful. That's because your teen will learn a valuable lesson and you don't have to be the heavy. The natural negative consequence does all the work for you. For example, if your teen impulsively spends all of his or her allowance money at the beginning of the week, there is no money left for weekend activities, like going to the movies. The lesson your teen learns is the value of saving.

Another example is keeping up with the laundry. If your teen is required to do his or her own laundry (and teenagers really should be required to do so) but doesn't keep up with the task, when your teen wants to wear a favorite shirt or pair of pants, it won't be clean. The lesson your teen learns here is the value of forethought and self-responsibility.

Of course, for natural consequences to work, you must refrain from "rescuing" your teen. You may occasionally want to offer helpful advice. But do so sparingly. A prophet is never welcomed in his or her own home. And it doesn't help matters, especially with teens, to be an "I told you so."

in these discussions. Doing so allows your teen to perceive that he or she has input into the norms that govern his or her behavior. This makes it less likely that your teen will view norms and rules as externally imposed, which increases the likelihood that they will behave in accordance with parental expectations. Plus, it increases the likelihood that teens will see their parents as effective sounding boards for the inner conflicts and tension that the teens experience.

You don't need to negotiate a behavioral contract for every problem behavior. Often, Grandma's Rule is sufficient. On the other hand, sometimes even behavioral contracting is not enough. If your teen's behavior problems are particularly severe, such as drug or alcohol abuse, running away from home, or violence, you should seek help from a psychologist or other mental health professional.

Parental response: Benign neglect.

Question Three: Does the behavior require that I intervene? Some annoying and troublesome behaviors require parental intervention, either because there is no naturally occurring negative consequence or the misbehavior is dangerous or destructive.

Examples include coming home after curfew, breaking household rules, failing to keep up with one's homework, and disobedience to a direct parental command. In such cases, you have to step up to the plate and respond with appropriate consequences. But make the punishment fit the crime.

If your teen breaks the household rule that says, "no TV until after homework is completed," restrict TV altogether for a couple of days, not for an entire month. If your teen fails to cut the grass as you asked, simply restrict his ability to be with friends until that chore is completed—don't add on lots of additional punishments. And have a sense of proportion. Coming home two hours after curfew requires more forceful discipline than coming home five minutes late.

If your attempts to alter illegal or self-destructive behavior are not immediately effective, seek professional help.

Parental response: Apply a logical consequence.

Question Four: Does this behavior happen repeatedly despite my intervention? Sometimes, despite having consistently applied a logical consequence, a particular troublesome behavior recurs with great frequency. If so, use active listening and behavioral contracting to negotiate solutions to problems.

Parental response: Use behavioral contracting. (See page 59.)

Question Five: Is the behavior illegal or self-destructive? If so, you need to lay down the law and enforce it. If your attempts to alter illegal or self-destructive behavior are not immediately effective, you should seek professional help.

Parental response: Take decisive action, including seeking professional counseling.

5

teen proofing your marriage

Trouble in a marriage tends to spill over into trouble in parent-teen relationships. The opposite is also true.

research consistently shows that couples in mutually satisfying marriages are more sensitive, involved, and responsive parents. Couples in unhappy marriages, on the other hand, are more likely to be inconsistent, over-controlling, and rejecting in their parenting.

It's like kicking the dog when you get home from a bad day at work. It may make you feel better (at least temporarily), but it doesn't solve the problem at the office. And it certainly doesn't do the dog any good. The same is true when marital problems spill over into relationships with our teenagers. It doesn't make the marital problems go away, and our teenagers don't like it one bit. And unlike most dogs, teenagers tend to bite back.

Parents who are unhappy with each other are less likely to encourage situations in which the other parent is positively involved with their teens. Instead, parents in troubled marriages frequently try to enlist their teens as allies in their fights with the other parent. Drawing teenagers into one's marital battles is never a good idea. Teenagers have enough to worry about without having to choose sides.

So if you want to have a good relationship with your teen, it helps to have a good relationship with your spouse. Plus, happy marriages provide a model for all sorts of good stuff for our kids, such as cooperation, sharing, selflessness, effective conflict resolution, and mutual support. If we want our kids to grow up to display these virtues toward others, it helps greatly if we demonstrate and provide an example of these virtues ourselves in the home.

Teenagers Are Hard on a Marriage

Unfortunately, not only can marital problems affect the parent-teen relationship, but parent-teen problems can also affect the marital relationship. In fact, only conflicts over family finances are more stressful on marriages than teenagers. As a result, marital satisfaction often drops when teenagers enter the picture. Fortunately, marital happiness tends to rebound after teenagers become young adults and (hopefully!) leave home. The trick is getting through the teenage years with your marriage intact.

Surviving the teenage years with your marriage intact isn't easy for several reasons. First, arguments about how to manage teenagers are a frequent source of marital conflict. When to extend privileges to teenagers, what kinds of household rules should be set, and when and how to punish teens are not always crystal clear. Because of the ambiguity inherent in parenting teens, these issues can easily become a source of argument and conflict between Mom and Dad. And everyone knows that arguments and conflict are not exactly conducive to marital happiness.

Indeed, if one is not careful, a vicious circle can develop: Teenagers cause stress in marriages, which makes parents less effective in parenting their teenagers. Less effective parenting means more parent-teen conflict and arguments. More parent-teen conflict and arguments place even more stress on the marriage. More stress on the marriage makes the parents even less effective. And on, and on, and on.

Second, having focused on their children for 12 years, some marital partners may have slowly drifted apart from each other emotionally. If so, the prospect of not having children around for very much longer can be threatening. These parents worry, "Without the kids around, who will

The Importance of Being Dad

It was not too long ago that developmental psychologist Michael Lamb, Ph.D., described fathers as the "forgotten contributors to child development." Today, there is an increasing recognition of the important role fathers play in the upbringing of their children, including teenagers. And not just as breadwinners, but as nurturers, disciplinarians, moral instructors, role models, and skill coaches.

One common mistake fathers make is believing that being a good dad is mostly about being a good disciplinarian. Certainly setting and enforcing clear limits is an important part of being a good dad. But fathers who are also affectionate, nurturing, available, and actively involved rear the most successful and well-adjusted teenagers. Furthermore, when dads are warm and affectionate, boys grow up with a healthier sense of their own masculinity and girls with a more secure sense of their femininity.

The best dads, then, are not those cold, distant martinets of yesteryear barking out orders and demanding slavish obedience, but those who combine warmth, affection, involvement, and availability with an ability to set and enforce clear limits.

there be to talk to?" Too often, parents have gotten out of the habit of enjoying just being with each other without the kids around.

Moms and Dads Parent Differently

Moms and dads tend to approach parenting differently. Not always, of course, and there are certainly exceptions, but the fact is that starting with the child's birth, moms and dads tend to approach this thing we call parenting in different ways.

We know, for example, that dads tend to be more physical with their children, whereas moms are more verbal. Dads like to throw their kids around like a sack of potatoes when they are little, whereas moms like to quietly read bedtime stories. We also know that when moms play with their kids, they frequently want them to learn something. Dads, it seems, just want to have a good time.

Perhaps the most important mom-dad difference in parenting teenagers is that dads are more encouraging of their teen's transition into adulthood.

Dads also tend to encourage more risk taking in their children, whereas moms encourage more caution. To observe this mom-dad difference one only need visit any playground in America to see fathers busily encouraging their children to "climb all the way to the top!" of the playground equipment while moms stand anxiously by urging them to "be careful!"

Mom-dad differences also show up when parenting teenagers. For example, moms, on average, tend to be more concerned with the process of being a teenager. Moms are very concerned about how their teenagers feel about things. Dads, on the other hand, are more likely to be concerned with outcomes during adolescence. Dads don't care so much how their teens feel about high school, for example, as they do about their teenagers' grades.

Perhaps the most important mom-dad difference in parenting teenagers is that dads are more encouraging of their teens' transition into adulthood. In fact, according to psychiatrist Frank Pittman, M.D., author of *Man Enough*, throughout history it has been fathers, or the community of fathers, that have tended to organize rituals proclaiming the entrance of their children (and boys especially) into the adult world. Moms, in contrast, tend to worry more about their "babies" wandering too far from the nest.

Differences in the way moms and dads approach parenting teenagers can become a source of conflict in a marriage. When moms and dads ask each other "Who's doing it right, you or me?" over such things as how much autonomy and risk taking ought to be allowed, far too frequently the answer each gives to the other is a forthright, "I am!"

Teenagers, who long ago learned the Machiavellian strategy of divide and conquer, love to take advantage of these interparental squabbles to get their way.

Unfortunately, when teens are successful in playing one parent off the other, it only adds further stress on the marriage.

Tips for Teenager Proofing Your Marriage

So what's a marriage to do? Here are some tips for teenager proofing your marriage. **Understand that teenagers can be stressful on a marriage.** Use this understanding to motivate you to redouble your efforts to keep your marriage strong and vital. This requires that you and your spouse communicate, communicate, communicate. And when you are done communicating, communicate some more. Remember: The two of you have a cunning nemesis in

keeping your marriage strong and vital

marital happiness is the certain hope of every couple approaching the altar. Here are some tips for actually achieving it.

Learn to listen. Talking *to* someone is different than talking *with* someone. If you want a happy marriage, learn to be a better listener than you are a talker.

Soften up requests. One surefire way to start an argument with a spouse is to demand he or she do something. Rather than saying, "I can't believe you haven't done the dishes yet. Do I have to do everything around here?" say, "Gee, I know you're tired, but the dishes really need to get done, and I have to finish the laundry. Do you think you could do the dishes?"

Respond with love and gentleness. When your spouse does make a request, respond positively without getting defensive. Rather than saying, "I work hard all day, and now I have to do the dishes too! What the heck do you do all day long?," say, "I can see you're really busy, so of course I'll help out." An important tip to the husbands: Women find men who vacuum incredibly sexy.

Give more than you receive. Many modern couples approach marriage as a 50/50 proposition. That's a sure path to marital unhappiness because as soon as one spouse feels he or she is doing 51 percent, that person begins to feel resentful. But if both of you strive to give 75 percent and expect only 25 percent in return, your focus will be on pleasing the other, not constantly testing the other's willingness to please you. So, for example, occasionally surprise your spouse by doing one of his or her chores and when asked why you did so, simply say, "Because I love you!"

Never argue when you're in the car. If we had a nickel for every evening ruined by a couple getting into an argument while in the car, we'd be relaxing in our posh villas in the Caribbean rather than writing this book. Make a simple rule that no arguments can occur in the car. You'll enjoy more evenings together that way, and you'll probably forget what it is you were arguing about by the time you get home.

Use affection and humor to defuse conflict. It's hard to stay angry at someone who walks over, hugs you and says, "I'm sorry, I'm being a jerk. I love you." You might also want to try coming up with a secret word that either of you can use early in an argument that signals to the other that you want the argument to immediately stop. Choosing a silly word to do this can help, a word like "snagglepuss" or "tuggly-wuggly," since it will inject a bit of humor into the situation. Then

your teen. If you are to succeed, you can't afford to spend your time bickering with your natural ally.

Practice an ounce of prevention. It's better than searching for a marital cure. Talk with your spouse in advance about household rules and the consequences when your teenager inevitably breaks them. Discussing these things in advance will greatly reduce the likelihood that you will find yourself arguing more with your spouse than your teenager when your teen arrives home several hours after curfew at 2 in the morning.

Learn to appreciate your differences. The fact that moms and dads often approach parenting differently does not mean that one is "right" and the other is

physically separate yourselves for a while to give each other time to calm down.

Don't pout. Many a marriage has gone down the drain because one or both partners pouted when confronted with conflict. Taking some time to cool off is not the same thing as pouting. All couples experience conflict and arguments. The key to marital happiness is not the amount of marital conflict, but how the couple manages it.

Rather than helping to resolve conflict, pouting interferes with effective conflict resolution. So if you're prone to pouting, know that doing so is one of the fastest routes to marital unhappiness—no matter how satisfying a good pout seems to feel at the time.

Say good stuff more than you say bad stuff. Nobody likes to be around someone who nags, belittles, or berates them. Get into the habit of giving lots of compliments and expressions of affection and appreciation. The more you give, the more you'll get.

Spend quality time alone together. Remember when you were first dating? You couldn't wait to be alone together. And when you were, you were polite, appreciative, and affectionate. No wonder your spouse fell in love with you! Become that person again and seek out opportunities to give each other your undivided attention. One way to find more time for each other is to turn off the TV. Johnny Carson once joked that his late night television show was a more effective contraceptive device than the Pill. He was right. Turn off the TV and you'll find more time to do things together.

> **Johnny Carson once joked that his late night television show was a more effective contraceptive device than the Pill.**

Mind your manners. When company comes over, even company we don't like very much, we put on our best manners. We say "please" and "thank you" and laugh at their jokes. Yet, when it comes to the most important people in the world—our spouses—we lapse into all sorts of ill-mannered and inconsiderate behavior. But good manners are critical to a successful marriage. So open doors and provide a helping hand to each other. Do show appreciation for the small gestures your spouse does for you. Showing good manners is an important way we communicate our respect for one another.

Enjoy each other. Nothing kills a marriage quicker than apathy. Do interesting and exciting things together. Develop a mutual hobby. Kidnap your spouse for a luncheon or dinner date. Have fun.

"wrong." Rather, teenagers do best when they experience the often complementary contributions of their moms and dads. Teens need someone to encourage risk taking, for example, but also someone to encourage caution.

Teens also need someone who is pushing them out of the nest, as well as someone who is reassuring them that the nest will always be there for them should they need to return.

Teens need someone who is pushing them out of the nest, as well as someone reassuring them that the nest will always be there for them.

Learn to appreciate and value mom-dad differences, and your marriage is much more likely to survive the teen years. Besides, it would get awfully boring if the two of you always did everything exactly the same. *Vive la différence!*

Rediscover each other. The teenage years are a time for dating. No, we're not referring to your teenager. We're talking about you and your spouse.

You spent the last 12 years or so spending time with the kids. Now that your kids, as teens, prefer the phone to you, go out with each other more. You deserve it. Rediscover each other, and romance will surely follow. Now, wouldn't that be nice!

What to Do If Your Marriage is in Trouble

Sometimes couples have drifted so far apart that dating yields not romance, but argument and conflict. This is a sign that your marriage is in trouble. If so, it is important not to give up too readily. The good news is that up to 80 percent of even troubled marriages can be saved. What is required is the motivation and commitment to do so.

When marital problems do occur, one common mistake couples make is believing that the most important thing is to resolve conflicts over specific parenting disagreements rather than the underlying marital problems. But focusing on arguments over specific parenting practices may only serve to mask underlying problems in the marital relationship. According to Jay Belsky, Ph.D., professor of Human Development at Pennsylvania State University in College Park, "Incompetent parenting is difficult to extinguish as long as the quality of the marital relationship is poor."

So if you and your spouse find yourselves arguing a lot about how to parent your teen, take this as a sign that your marriage may be in trouble. If it is, take heart. With help, you and your spouse can fall in love with each other again.

Repairing troubled marriages does takes commitment. If you're having trouble generating that commitment, consider how much more difficult things would be if, in addition to everything else your teen has to cope with, he or she must also cope with divorce.

We're not suggesting that you "stay together for the sake of the kids at all costs." But we are suggesting that if you are experiencing marital problems, you use the fact that you have children to motivate yourselves to do everything you possibly can to repair and revitalize your marriage.

How Divorce Affects Teenagers

There's no easy way of getting around it. Divorce is hard on teenagers, and for several reasons.

Reason Number One: When parents divorce, both moms and dads become less effective in their parenting, at least for a time, and any parenting problems that existed before the divorce tend to become exacerbated by the divorce.

In particular, following a divorce, parents often become less likely to monitor the behavior of their adolescents, less involved in decisions regarding their teenagers, more willing to leave a teenager home alone, less likely to help with homework, and more permissive in their parenting.

In other words, following a divorce, many parents are so preoccupied with their own issues and concerns that they have less energy to invest in the critical task of parenting their teens.

Reason Number Two: Teenagers, despite reassurances to the contrary, tend to experience divorce as personal rejection. "You're not just leaving Mom," they reason, "you're also leaving me." Furthermore, many teens also believe the divorce is somehow their fault. "If only I didn't misbehave as much," teenagers frequently surmise, "you wouldn't be getting a divorce."

The reason children often blame themselves for parental divorce is that the most visible arguments in troubled marriages are often about parenting the kids. According to noted divorce researcher Judith Wallerstein, Ph.D., children, including teens, are often "blissfully unaware" of other aspects of troubled marriages. So when their parents approach them with the news of an impending divorce, teens often see this as a result of trouble they have caused.

Reason Number Three: The relationship with one's father seems to be particularly affected by divorce. At ages 12 to 16, 32 percent of children from divorced families reported having a poor relationship with their fathers, according to a national longitudinal study by

Nicholas Zill, Ph.D., and his colleagues at Child Trends, Inc., a Washington, D.C., based research and consulting firm.

Evidence is overwhelming that when children grow up without an involved, committed, and responsible father in their lives, they are at greater risk for a host of negative developmental outcomes, including educational failure, juvenile delinquency, depression, and early and promiscuous sexual activity.

Reason Number Four: Divorce often leads to other destabilizing stressors in a teenager's life. For example, adolescents from divorced homes move more frequently,

Denying that a teenager experiences emotional distress following divorce may only serve to add to the stress the teenager feels.

leading to more stress and less stability in neighborhood relationships. Following a divorce, teens may also withdraw from friends due to depression, or, even worse, may become attracted to deviant peer groups as a way of expressing their anger about the divorce.

Divorce Is Hard on Teens

Not surprisingly, teens who experience the divorce of their parents are at high risk for behavioral and emotional problems. In particular, they are more likely to be sexually active, report being more susceptible to peer pressure, and are more likely to commit delinquent acts.

Teenagers' physical health also suffers after a divorce. When parents divorce, teens often start substituting snacks for meals. In a national sample of 1,310 teens aged 11 to 18, adolescents living in a single-parent household were significantly more likely to form an inconsistent meal pattern, and the meals they did eat tended to include more fat and less nutrition.

Boys seem to be particularly affected by divorce, especially when they disengage from the family and associate with an antisocial peer group. But girls are affected by divorce as well, although somewhat differently. The rule of thumb is this: Boys externalize the stress of a divorce whereas girls internalize the stress. This means that following a divorce boys are more at risk for conduct problems and juvenile delinquency, and girls are more at risk for depression, eating disorders, and promiscuous sexual activity.

This does not mean, of course, that every teenager who experiences divorce will develop problems. Many teens adjust to their parents' divorce without experiencing significant behavioral or emotional problems. But divorce does place teens at higher risk for such difficulties. And the absence of overt behavioral problems does not mean the teenager is not experiencing internal distress. In fact, denying that a teenager experiences emotional distress following divorce may only serve to add to the stress the teenager feels.

How to Talk to a Teenager About Divorce

Perhaps the most difficult thing any couple may ever do is tell their children that they are getting a divorce. While we hope that the information in this book will help you keep your marriage strong and vital, we understand that divorce is sometimes the best option for you, your spouse, and your children. Here are some ways to talk with your teens if, in fact, you are getting a divorce.

Do it together. If at all possible, both parents need to be a part of the discussion. This will not be easy. But talking to teenagers together about the impending divorce will make it less likely that they will feel placed "in the middle" or forced to choose sides. It also makes it less likely that you will be tempted to say bad things about the other parent.

Pick the right time. You should have your teenager's undivided attention. Tell your teenager that the two of you have something important to discuss with him or her. Ask that the teenager offer a good time for talking. Pick a neutral place, and make sure there are no distractions, like the TV. Take the phone off the hook.

Be brief. Short conversations may be more helpful than longer ones, which often are interpreted by teenagers as lectures.

Be prepared for a nonresponse. As a self-protection mechanism, some

help for the divorcing (or divorced) parent

Resources for parents and teens:

Association of Family and Conciliation Courts
329 West Wilson St.
Madison, WI 53703-3612
608/251-4001
www.afccnet.org
Publishes a Directory of Parent Education Programs as well as a series of pamphlets for divorcing (and divorced) families, including *Joint Custody: A New Way of Being Related, Twenty Questions Divorcing Parents Ask About Their Children, Child Support, Child Visitation/Parent Access—A Relationship That Lasts Forever*, and *Child & Divorce*.

Rainbows
1111 Tower Rd.
Schaumburg, IL 60173
800/266-3206
www.rainbows.org
A national organization dedicated to helping children and teens cope with divorce. It serves more than 700,000 youth through more than 5,000 community-based sites in the U.S. There is no charge for teenagers' participation, but parental permission is required.

Books to read:

In the Name of the Child: A Developmental Approach to Understanding and Helping Children of Conflict and Violent Divorce
by Janet R. Johnston and Vivienne Roseby
New York: Free Press (1997)

Difficult Questions Kids Ask About Divorce
by M. Schneider and J. Zuckerman
New York: Fireside Press (1996)

Families Apart: Ten Keys to Successful Co-Parenting
by Melinda Blau
New York: Perigee (1993)

Child Custody: Building Parenting Agreements That Work
by Mimi Lyster
Berkeley, CA: Nolo Press (1996)

teenagers react to the news with a shrug of the shoulders and a curt, "Whatever," or "That's your problem. I'm going out." But don't cut off discussion if your teenager wants to continue talking. Let your teen be your guide as to the appropriate amount of discussion he or she can handle.

Never speak ill of the other parent. Don't use this as an occasion for more argument with your spouse or to establish blame. If necessary, rehearse what each of you is going to say so as to minimize the possibility that the discussion will degenerate into mutual name-calling.

Don't let your teen take on guilt. Make sure your teen understands that he or she is not the problem. One of the most frequent beliefs of children of divorce is

staying in touch

If you are a noncustodial parent, the hardest part is staying in touch with your kids. Yet research consistently shows that one of the best predictors of a child's well-being following a divorce is whether or not both parents maintain a strong relationship with the child.

Here are some tips for being a good noncustodial parent:

Let your teens know that you think about them every day. Make sure your teens know that despite the fact that you do not live with them, they are a constant part of your daily life. Let your teens know that you have their photographs up on the walls of your home and office. You could say, for example, "I was looking at your picture today on my desk at work, and just wanted to call to say 'hi.'" Also, invite your son or daughter to send you photocopies of important papers, like report cards or certificates of achievement, so that you can put them up on your refrigerator and walls.

Be a pen pal. Phone calls are good, but letter writing is even better. Letter writing has the advantage over phone calls in that letters can be transformed into permanent treasures which your kids can re-read whenever they need a noncustodial parent "fix." It's helpful to write letters whether you live across the street, across town, or across the country. And encourage them to write back by providing them with addressed and stamped return envelopes. Their letters to you can be helpful when you're the one who needs a kid "fix."

Become comfortable with the Internet. Many teenagers have difficulty having long intimate conversations with their parents over the phone. The Internet is better. Sending e-mail back and forth gives both of you time to formulate questions and responses.

The Internet also offers the advantage of allowing your kids to decide when it is a good time for them to communicate with you. This gives them a measure of control, which can be helpful for them in coping with their own feelings of loss. If there is a fax machine in your teenagers' home, consider sending them a daily fax telling them what you did each day.

Pursue shared interests. Sharing a hobby or sport interest helps to solidify a relationship and provides assurances of time spent together. Even if you are not always doing the activity together, it gives you something to talk about when you are together.

that they somehow caused the divorce. This is because one of the most frequent, and visible, sources of conflict in a marriage is children. Reassure them that there is nothing they did to cause the divorce to happen.

Reassure your teen. Make sure your teen knows that you are divorcing each other, not the teen. Fear of abandonment is perhaps the greatest fear of most children who experience divorce. Explain to your teenager that you have developed, or will be developing, a coparenting plan to make sure that both of you will continue to be involved in your teen's life.

Be certain, not uncertain. The most frequent fantasy of children of divorce is that their parents will reconcile. While some divorcing couples do eventually

Keep your commitments. Every child of divorce, even teenagers, struggles with whether or not his or her parents will eventually abandon him or her. Don't give your teenager reason to believe this will happen by making promises you don't keep. So if you say you are going to come by the softball game after school, make sure you do so. Most importantly, make scheduled visitation times the very last thing you cancel.

Don't play Santa Claus. Avoid bringing presents or giving lots of money every time you see your teenager. A simple walk to the park or cooking a meal together oftentimes has more impact than big production days. Your teens need your time, not your money.

Continue to act like a parent. Part of the work of being a parent is setting and enforcing clear limits. Teenagers don't like that part, but it is essential to their well-being. Sometimes noncustodial parents are so afraid of losing their teenagers' love following a divorce that they become reluctant to discipline them. But the divorce didn't lessen your teens' need for limits. In fact, it probably has even increased it.

> If you say you are going to come by the softball game after school, make sure you do so.

Don't let divorce become an excuse factory for your teen. Some teens may begin to cite the divorce as an excuse for unacceptable behavior. But while empathizing with their feelings about the divorce is important, so is the need to continue to set and enforce clear limits. So don't shrug off your teenager's sudden failing grades as simply a reaction to the divorce. Your teen needs you now more than ever to provide him or her with guidance and high expectations for appropriate behavior, as well as emotional support.

Support and honor the custodial parent. One of the hardest things about being a divorced parent is to work with your former spouse to raise your teenagers well. It is also the single most important thing you have to do. Continued conflict between divorced parents is the best predictor of poor outcomes for children of divorce. Learn to keep any lingering angry feelings in check. By keeping hostility and conflict between you and your former spouse to an absolute minimum, you will benefit your teenagers greatly.

reconcile, it is better not to wave this possibility in front of your teenager when discussing an impending divorce.

Be concrete, not vague. Teenagers are very egocentric. They will want to know, "How will this affect me?" Explain to them how this will—and will not—affect their daily lives. Explain to them, for example, where each parent is going to live, where they are going to live, where they will be going to school, and whether they will be able to continue to play soccer or pursue other interests.

It is best to strive for as much stability in teenagers' lives as possible both during and following the divorce. That's why, if at all possible, it is almost always

Although parents may feel a sense of relief when the decision to divorce has been finalized, this is an unlikely reaction on the part of teenagers.

best for teenagers to stay in the family home and neighborhood where they have access to peer and other support networks, and can continue to pursue current interests and activities.

Give your teen an opportunity to vent his or her feelings. Most children, when first approached by their parents about divorce, experience an extraordinary array of feelings, including sadness, anger, and denial. Allow your teen to express these emotions and do express your empathy. Don't belittle or try to deny the validity of these emotions, as this will only make your teen feel worse.

If, however, your teen's behavior begins to escalate to the point where he or she becomes dangerous or destructive, set a firm limit on this behavior by saying, for example, "I understand that you are upset by this, but we will not allow you to throw things."

Don't insist that your teenager's reactions be the same as yours. Be prepared for the fact that your teenager's reaction to the divorce is likely to be very different from yours. Although parents may feel a sense of relief when the decision to divorce has been finalized, this is an unlikely reaction on the part of teenagers. Don't pressure them into seeing the divorce as a "good" thing.

Answer your teens' questions as honestly as you can. Teens are more likely than younger children to ask you questions about your marriage and the divorce. Be as honest and straightforward as you can in answering their questions. But being honest doesn't mean saying hurtful things about the other parent like, "We're getting a divorce because your father's a drunk," or "We're getting a divorce because your mom had an adulterous affair." Be honest, but discreet. Your teenagers don't need to know the gory details.

Offer to talk more later. Let your teenager know that you are available to talk whenever he or she feels the need. In fact, you should anticipate having to have several talks, not just one. Don't assume teenagers will be able to resolve all their feelings in one conversation. Multiple conversations give teens time in between to consolidate information and resolve feelings. And not all follow-up conversations need to be planned. Sometimes the most meaningful conversations will occur when driving your teen to school or the mall. Look for these informal times to continue the conversation.

Seek professional help if necessary. Some teenagers react violently to the news of an impending divorce. If you see signs that your teenager is using alcohol or illegal drugs, is having suicidal thoughts, or may be planning to run away from home, seek professional help immediately.

Divorce is a very stressful time for everyone. Despite whatever conflicts have led to your decision to divorce, the two of you must work together as a team to minimize the consequences of divorce on your children—both during and after the divorce. If you are having trouble doing this on your own, we strongly suggest you seek assistance from a divorce mediator skilled in the development of coparenting plans—a written agreement as to how the two of you will work together as a parenting team following the divorce.

Most of all, live up to your coparenting plan. Reassurance never really reassures unless it is backed up by action. Telling teenagers that both of you will continue to be a part of their lives after the divorce is not sufficient; you must make sure that it actually happens. That is the hardest part of all. It is also the most important.

Helping Teenagers Cope with Divorce

If you are going through a divorce, or are already divorced, here are some suggestions for helping your teenagers cope.

Ensure that your teen is able to maintain a relationship with both parents. Research consistently shows that following a divorce, children who maintain good relationships with both parents have the most positive outcomes.

Consequently, except in cases of domestic violence or child abuse, the most important goal of any divorce proceeding is not division of property, but ensuring that the children continue to have the opportunity to have a close relationship with both parents. One way to do this is to pursue custody mediation rather than custody litigation.

There is evidence that both parents are more likely to remain involved with their children following divorce if they participate in a process designed to improve coparenting, such as custody mediation, rather than a process such as litigation that may only further strain the relationship between former spouses.

Don't leave success to chance—develop an explicit coparenting plan. It is important that this plan be written and explicit. Not only should the coparenting plan indicate custody and visitation arrangements, but also such things as curfews, homework expectations, and ways of communicating with each other about infringements of household rules.

Remember, consistency is a key to effectively parenting teens. When parents live in different households, consistency is doubly hard to maintain. To do so, you are going to need a written plan.

Minimize conflict and work as a team. We know. If you could work effectively as a team, you might not have gotten a divorce in the first place. But it is important to your teenager's well-being that the two of you strive to set aside the conflict that caused the divorce and work together to parent your teenager well.

Be faithful to your coparenting plan. If you didn't develop a coparenting plan during the divorce process, now is the time to do so. If you are having difficulty developing a coparenting plan, you may need to contact a professional mediator experienced in these issues to help you with this process.

If you find yourself angry, spiteful, or upset with your divorced partner, take a moment and see this experience through the eyes of your teenager.

Maintain a positive attitude toward the noncustodial parent. In far too many instances of divorce, rather than respecting and supporting the other parent, divorced parents often say mean and nasty things about each other. If you are divorced, this is the worst thing you could possibly do—no matter what the provocation.

Most divorcing parents promise their teenagers that although they are divorcing each other, neither is divorcing the teen. The best way to prove you meant this is to respect and support the other parent, and especially the other parent's right to have a close relationship with your teen.

See the world through your teenager's eyes. Whenever you find yourself angry, spiteful, or upset with your divorced partner, take a moment and see this experience through the eyes of your teenager. Wouldn't you really rather that your teen see you and your former spouse cooperating and supporting each other than saying mean and hurtful things about each other? Reflecting on the impact your behavior can have on your teen can be immensely helpful in keeping your own behavior under control.

Give out lots of hugs. Sometimes we are tempted to believe that teenagers don't need as much love, time, and attention as younger children. But they do.

In fact, the stress of divorce makes these needs even greater. So remember to spend time with your teens and tell them how much you love them. Giving your teens time and attention during and following a divorce will help reassure them that there is never any danger of your falling out of love with them.

Adjusting to a Stepfamily

Perhaps the most difficult adjustment any teenager can be asked to make is to become a member of a stepfamily.

Reason Number One: Many children harbor the fantasy that their parents will reconcile and get remarried. The formation of a stepfamily dashes that fantasy.

Losing this hope can sometimes lead to a great deal of anger and resentment directed at the stepparent.

Reason Number Two: When stepfamilies form, parents often act as if the marriage ceremony instantly transformed them into a new, happy, fully functioning family unit—a kind of Brady Bunch II.

Unfortunately, it takes a lot of time for every member of the family to adjust to this new living arrangement. Pretending there are not going to be difficulties along the way can put a great deal of pressure on everyone to act "as if"—as if there were no ambiguities in roles, as if there were no problems, as if they were the Brady Bunch! You need to realize that there will be bumps along the way.

Reason Number Three: A stepchild may lose his or her treasured and familiar position within the family. The oldest child may suddenly find himself or herself with one or more older siblings. The "baby" of the family may suddenly have one or more younger brothers or sisters. Losing one's familiar role within a family can cause tremendous confusion and stress.

Reason Number Four: As discussed in Chapter 3, the primary task of the teenage years is the search for self: Who am I? What kind of person do I want to be? How do I fit into the rest of the world? These are hard enough questions for any teen to struggle with under even the best of circumstances.

This struggle is made all the more difficult when a whole other set of questions is added to the list: How do I fit into this "new" family? What does it mean to be a stepsister or stepbrother? How do I relate to this stepmother or stepfather?

Here are some suggestions for helping teenagers adjust to becoming a member of a stepfamily:

Don't insist that teenagers call their stepparent "Mom" or "Dad." Teenagers know the difference between biological parents and stepparents. Teens often view "Mom" and "Dad" as terms reserved for their biological parents.

Things will go a lot smoother if you respect their wish to reserve these terms for

Expect the adjustment period to take a long time. It often takes from three to five years after remarriage to adjust to a new stepparent and changes in household rules and chores.

their biological parents. Find some other way to have your teenagers refer to their stepparent. Of course, if they want to call their stepparent "Mom" or "Dad," you needn't discourage it. Just don't get offended if they don't.

Establish a relationship with stepchildren first. Worry about parenting second. Functioning as a friend or "camp counselor" initially, rather than trying to discipline or control stepchildren, can help their acceptance of the stepparent, according to Dr. James H. Bray, Ph.D., associate director of Family Psychology Programs at Baylor College of Medicine in Houston, Texas. This is especially so for teenagers, who are often tempted to get into all sorts of mischief as a way of rebelling against a stepparent's attempts to discipline. Instead, have the biological parent play disciplinarian for the early part of the remarriage. The job of the stepparent is to work on building a relationship with his or her stepchildren.

Don't insist that stepchildren be physically affectionate. Like all parents, stepparents want to express affection by hugging and kissing their kids. However, stepchildren—and especially teenagers—frequently feel uncomfortable with such displays of physical affection. It is better to concentrate on using praise and compliments as a means to communicate your affection for your stepchildren.

Support your stepchildren's continued relationship with the non-custodial, biological parent. Research consistently shows that children do best following a divorce when they continue to have a relationship with both their biological mother and biological father. One of the most difficult requirements of stepparenting is actively encouraging a close relationship between your stepchildren and the noncustodial, biological parent. It's also one of the most important requirements of successful stepparenting.

One way to help is to avoid using the prefix "ex." Your former spouse may be your "ex-husband" or "ex-wife," but there is nothing "ex" about your teenager's relationship to the noncustodial parent. Teenagers don't want to hear their dad or mom (and siblings that don't live with them) spoken about in that way.

Don't expect stepsiblings to automatically get along. Expect some conflict and jealousy between stepsiblings. The root problem of sibling rivalry in stepfamilies is the same as that for sibling rivalry between natural siblings: competition. Who gets the most attention? Who is the favorite? Who gets better

help for the stepparent

Here are some good resources:

Stepfamily Foundation, Inc.
333 West End Avenue
New York, NY 10023
212/877-3244
website: www.stepfamily.org

The Stepfamily Association of America
650 J Street, Suite 205
Lincoln, NE 68508
800/735-0329
website: www.stepfam.org

Some good books to read include:

Living in a Stepfamily Without Getting Stepped On
by K. Leman
Nashville: Nelson Publishers (1994)

Developing Healthy Stepfamilies: Twenty Families Tell Their Stories
by P. Kelley
Binghamton, NY: Haworth (1994)

Stepchild-by-Stepparenting: A Guide to Successful Living with a Blended Family
by J. Eckler
Cincinnati: Betterway Books (1993)

Stepfamily Realities: How to Overcome Difficulties and Have a Happy Family
by M. Newman
Oakland, CA: New Harbinger (1994)

Stepparent Is Not a Bad Word: Advice and Perspectives on Parenting Your Stepchildren
by D. Nowell
Nashville: Nelson Publishers (1994)

stuff? These are questions that only intensify in stepsibling relationships.

To help, ensure everyone understands what are acceptable ways of expressing conflict and what are not. And acknowledging the reality of tension and conflict between stepsiblings is better than trying to drive it underground.

Communicate, communicate, communicate with your spouse. Children are stressful on a relationship. That's why in most cases we're only allowed to acquire them one at a time. When a stepfamily is formed, suddenly there may be a number of "new" children. This is hard on the marital relationship. In fact, remarriages are quicker to break up than first marriages. The best way to prevent this from happening is to work especially hard at keeping lines of communication open between you and your new spouse.

Expect the adjustment period to take a long time. It often takes from three to five years after remarriage to adjust to a new stepparent and changes in household rules and chores, according to research by Mavis Heatherington, Ph.D., professor of psychology at the University of Virginia in Charlottesville. This is much longer than most stepparents expect it to take. So don't get too discouraged by the inevitable ups and downs of stepparenting.

Final Thoughts

The teenage years can be difficult even under the best of circumstances—and the best circumstance is certainly growing up with the love and devotion of one's married parents.

This doesn't mean that divorced, unwed, or stepparents can not raise teenagers successfully. Of course they can. Many do. But it is harder. On everyone.

Pointing out that divorce or stepparenting can cause significant, and at times even overwhelming, stress on teenagers should never be used as a weapon merely to produce guilt in already divorced parents or stepparents. But knowing that divorce and stepfamilies can be stressful to teenagers ought to be used by married couples to help them sustain the motivation to keep their marriages strong and vital despite the strains that adolescents can place on a marriage. It is our hope that this chapter has provided some useful ideas for doing so.

Moving through the teen years is one of life's most challenging journeys. The pathway is sometimes rocky and the ultimate destination frequently unknown. Fortunately, most teenagers get through this journey just fine. But for the journey to go well, teenagers need a secure home port from which to travel on their journey to adulthood. Providing that secure home port is one of the most important things parents can do to help their teens on their way.

6

A-Z problems & solutions

For the most part teenagers are healthy. But what if it's prom night and there's a zit on your nose?

Parents have their hands full with a teenager in the house. The preadolescent and teen years are a time of monumental change. Nature has programmed in a whole host of physical, mental, and emotional turns in the road. Even when everything is chugging along exactly as it should, the typical family hits rough spots. Problems can and do develop on a fairly regular basis. That's where this chapter comes in. This handy A–Z reference guide will help you find solutions to the most common problems that teens and their parents face.

How can you help your teen control a bad case of acne? What do you do with a teenager who refuses to eat? Or with an overweight teenager? If your teenager looks at you and says, "I feel so ugly I could die," you need to have some idea how to help heal that low self-esteem. Please understand that while this chapter provides some practical and quick solutions, it can't solve more serious problems—such as alcohol abuse or clinical depression. It does offer some guidelines and insights, however, about when you need to seek professional help.

Acne

If acne flared up, say, on the small of the back, it would be an easy disease to ignore. After all, it isn't life threatening, and it doesn't really hurt all that much. But acne is a nasty sort of problem, in that it attacks the face—the part of a person that's most important for self-esteem, the part that presents the inner person to the outer world.

A case of acne, left untreated, can erode a teen's self-confidence and can lead to frustration and even depression. Fortunately, acne can be treated. No matter how bad the case, dermatologists say that your teenager never has to suffer a "pizza face," and that there is absolutely no reason for permanent pitting or scarring.

What is It?

Acne is a disease that causes the hair follicles in the skin to become plugged. Here's how it works. The sebaceous glands, little multilobed glands in the skin, produce an oil called sebum. These glands are attached to a hair follicle—an opening in the skin with a tiny hair. Normally, the sebum travels up the hair follicle and out onto the skin's surface.

But for many kids, this smooth and simple process just goes haywire. During adolescence hormonal changes stimulate the sebaceous glands to produce more sebum. The main hormonal culprit is androgen, a male sex hormone present in both boys and girls. But the female hormone progesterone also plays a role in the acne problems that girls encounter.

So, a teenager's sebaceous glands are pumping out a lot of extra, oily sebum. At the same time the glands are going into overdrive, the inner surface of the hair follicle also is changing.

Before androgen began its terrorist action against the skin, hair follicles worked just fine. Cells inside the follicle shed gradually and moved up to the skin's surface. But no more. Now the dead cells slough off rapidly. And they're sticky. They clump together.

When these sticky, extra cells mix with oily, extra sebum—gunk!—the follicle becomes plugged.

Add to this unpleasant situation a bacteria called *Propionibacterium acnes*,

(*P. acnes*) which is always present on the skin. This bacteria invades the clogged follicle. It just thrives on the sebum-cell mix and multiplies rapidly. *P. acnes* produces chemicals that cause inflammation in the follicle and the surrounding skin. And the result is a pimple.

Since most of the sebaceous glands are found on the face, neck, chest, shoulders, and back, that's where acne breakouts are found, too.

Sweat, dirt, oil, and oily cosmetics also contribute to the development of acne.

Who Gets It?

Almost all teenagers experience acne to some extent. Acne is an equal-opportunity affliction, affecting both boys and girls. Boys, however, usually develop a more severe, longer-lasting condition. Girls, on the other hand, can suffer breakouts during their monthly periods and from using oily makeup.

How Do You Treat It?

To begin treating acne, suggest that your teen:

- Wash his or her face twice a day with a mild soap, then gently pat it dry
- Avoid scrubbing the face or using "facial scrubs" (Such aggressive action irritates the skin.)
- Avoid squeezing or picking at pimples
- Keep hands (or any object) off the face

Over-the-Counter Help Next, try medication. Acne treatments are available over the counter or by prescription. All of them work by reducing sebum production, by speeding up skin-cell turnover, or by fighting bacterial infection, or any combination of these three methods.

Two OTC standbys are benzoyl peroxide and salicylic acid. They usually help mild cases. Ask your pharmacist to recommend a product containing either of these ingredients.

Benzoyl peroxide works by destroying *P. acnes* bacteria. Your teenager will see results in about two weeks. Salicylic acid helps unclog pores by slowing down the abnormal shedding of cells. It prevents new pimples from forming. It, too, takes a couple of weeks to work.

Even after the all-clear, your teen will have to continue to use either medication every day to prevent flare-ups.

Prescription Drugs Your doctor has a veritable arsenal to fight acne, ranging from powerful lotions to antibiotics, and even contraceptives. (Don't panic. Birth control pills have the effect of regulating hormones. Prescribed as a skin treatment, they don't have to send a message that sexual activity is OK.) Here's an overview of the kind of prescription drugs that may get called into the antiacne battle:

Vitamin A derivatives: One of the most commonly prescribed

Doctor:

Help your teenager to save face by seeing a doctor when:

- Over-the-counter products don't do the job
- Large, painful bumps appear
- Scars or pits begin to form
- Large, dark patches appear after pimples have started to heal
- Acne interferes with your teen's quality of life

How to Apply Acne Medication:

Acne medications don't just treat the pimples and blackheads of today. They help to prevent the lesions of tomorrow.

If your teen is simply dabbing medicine on current spots, he or she is not getting the full benefit of the treatment.

Instead, be sure your teen applies medicine to an entire area that breaks out. For some, that means covering the whole face, neck, chest, shoulders, and back.

medications is a product containing Vitamin A acid (tretinoin or retinoic acid). This drug works best on moderate-to-severe acne. It helps to unclog pores and slows down the abnormally fast cell shedding in the hair follicle. Vitamin A acids are also available as an oral medication, which also helps slow down sebum production.

Retinoids can be used in combination with other acne preparations, such as benzoyl peroxide or oral antibiotics.

Accutane, another form of Vitamin A acid, is prescribed for the treatment of cystic acne. It's a powerful drug that can cause birth defects. It should not be used by anyone who is pregnant or who might become pregnant. (If your daughter takes this drug it is vitally important that she understands this.)

Don't Blame Chocolate

Chocolate is innocent. Oh, it may make you fat, if you eat enough of it. But it doesn't cause pimples.

Dermatologists tell us that acne has nothing to do with your teenager's diet. Chocolate chips do not, through some weird wizardry, turn into zits. The butter your teenager melts on an English muffin does not later ooze from his or her pores as excess sebum.

So, why are we even saying this? For years popular "wisdom" had it that chocolate contributed to acne. Some doctors even thought this was true. And many's the poor kid who's refused (or guiltily indulged in) this wonderful treat with an eye to the mirror.

That said, some individuals who have acne still claim that there is a correlation between what they eat and a breakout of pimples. Everyone's body is different. If any food, including chocolate, seems to lead to skin problems for your teenager, then by all means, do make the necessary dietary modifications.

But for most kids, food is not a contributing factor. Simply provide a normal, balanced diet, such as that described in Chapter 2.

Antibiotics: These germ fighters are also part of the usual armament against acne. They can be used topically or taken orally. They work by obliterating *P. acnes* from the skin. Topical antibiotics are less effective than oral simply because they can penetrate only a limited distance into the skin. Oral antibiotics circulate throughout the body, even into the sebaceous glands. Even so, antibiotics can take weeks—even months—to clear up the skin. They are usually prescribed in combination with other acne medications.

Oral antibiotics, because they are systemic, have more side effects than the topical version. (For that reason, they should not be taken by anyone who is pregnant or who might become pregnant. They also reduce the effectiveness of some oral contraceptives.)

Oral contraceptives: Birth control pills contain female hormones and work on acne by counteracting the effects of androgen. They can be prescribed only for girls. Different brands of oral contraceptives contain female hormones in different combinations, so one type may be more effective for an individual than another. An oral contraceptive called Ortho Tri-Cyclen has been shown to improve acne, according to the Food and Drug Administration.

Corticosteroids: These powerful anti-inflammatory drugs are injected directly into severely inflamed acne nodules by a doctor.

ADHD (Attention Deficit Hyperactivity Disorder)

do you have a teenager who has trouble paying attention at school and is easily distracted by background noises or activity? Does your teenager act impulsively without thinking through the consequences? Does your teen have difficulty waiting his or her turn? Does your teen frequently interrupt others or shout out answers in class?

All of this may sound like a fairly typical teen. And just about every teen displays at least some of these characteristics from time to time. But if these traits persist, then you could very well be dealing with a teenager who has attention deficit hyperactivity disorder—often known simply by its acronym, ADHD.

The primary symptoms of ADHD are inattention and impulsivity beginning by age 7 and displayed on a regular basis at home and at school. Over 2.5 million

Many, but not all, kids with ADHD also display high levels of activity. These kids are frequently described as fidgety and always on the go.

children in the U.S. have been diagnosed with ADHD, or about 3 to 5 percent of all school-aged children.

Many, but not all, kids with ADHD also display high levels of activity. These kids are frequently described as fidgety, restless, and always on the go. Many with ADHD are also chronically noncompliant with the instructions and directions of teachers and parents. Sometimes their noncompliance is due to "forgetting" or inattention. Other times it is due to their being oppositional.

For many years, it was thought that children with ADHD gradually outgrow their ADHD as they become teenagers. And some do. But we now know that for many persons with ADHD this is not the case.

Although the severity of the symptoms often decreases as children with ADHD enter their teenage years, most continue to have significant problems with both paying attention and delaying impulses well into adolescence. And many continue to display symptoms even into adulthood.

Dealing with ADHD

Treatment for teenagers with ADHD usually is comprised of some combination of medication, a technique known as behavioral contracting, and instruction in self-control techniques.

Typical ADHD Medications The most common medications prescribed for treating ADHD are methylphenidate (often referred to by its trade name Ritalin) and d-amphetamine (often referred to by its trade name Dexedrine). These medications are helpful in about 70 percent of cases in reducing the primary symptoms of inattention and impulsivity. They do, however, have the potential for side effects, such as loss of appetite, insomnia, and stomach pains.

In very high doses, they also have the potential for abuse. This is especially the case with teenagers. There have been reports of teens snorting or ingesting large doses in order to get high. No teenager should be prescribed these medications without first having undergone a comprehensive psychological assessment and medical exam.

If your teenager has any history of problems with illegal drug use, make sure you share this information with the doctor treating your teen for ADHD.

And don't be fooled into believing that simply taking medications is enough. There are other factors that need to be considered in treating ADHD.

Behavioral Contracting Teens with ADHD need to learn how to control their own behavior, not simply rely upon a pill to do this for them.

Parents can help teens with ADHD develop self-control with a technique known as behavioral contracting. (For details on this important parenting tool, see page 59 in Chapter 4). It is often helpful for teens with ADHD to have a daily schedule, waking up at the same time, eating at the same time, doing homework at the same time, and so forth.

At school, teens with ADHD can be helped by being placed in small group settings, and through the use of something called a daily home report card. Daily home report cards entail having your teen record homework assignments for each class on a daily basis and then having each teacher initial each assignment indicating that the student has written the homework assignment down correctly. Parents then review the daily home report card each day after their teen arrives home from school.

If your teenager's problems are particularly severe (such as when drug or alcohol abuse is involved, or if your teenager has a history of running away from home), then you will probably need the help of a psychologist or other mental health professional to adequately address your concerns about these problems.

Learning Disabilities

Teens with attention deficit hyperactivity disorder (ADHD) frequently, but not always, also have learning disabilities. A learning disability is a neurological condition that makes it difficult for someone to process certain types of information efficiently.

An indication that your teen may have a learning disability is a history of significant underachievement at school that can not be explained by low intelligence, lack of educational opportunities, emotional problems such as depression, or family stress such as divorce. Early warning signs often include difficulty with organization and memory.

A learning disability is particularly suspected if these problems manifest in a core academic area. There are specific names for the condition that causes problems in each area. The disorder that creates problems in reading in known as dyslexia. The one that causes problems in written language is know as dysgraphia. And

For More Information
on ADHD

To find out more about attention deficit hyperactivity disorder (ADHD), you can contact the following organizations:

Attention Deficit Disorders Association
9930 Johnnycake Ridge, Suite 3E
Mentor, OH 44060
440/350-9595

CH.A.D.D. (Children and Adults with Attention Deficit Disorder)
8181 Professional Place
Landover, MD
800/233-4050

Some good books for parents and teenagers with ADHD are:

ADHD: Questions and Answers for Parents
by Gregory S. Greenberg, Ph.D., and Wade F. Horn, Ph.D.
Champaign, IL: Research Press (1991)

I Would If I Could: A Teenager's Guide to ADHD/Hyperactivity
by Michael Gordon, Ph.D.
DeWitt, NY: GSI Publications (1993)

Putting Yourself in Their Shoes: Understanding Teenagers with Attention Deficit Hyperactivity Disorder
by Harvey C. Parker, Ph.D.
Plantation, FL: Specialty Press, Inc. (1999)

the condition that gets in the way of doing arithmetic is known as dyscalculia.

If you suspect that your teenager has a learning disability, the best way to find out is to have your child tested by a qualified school or clinical psychologist. Ask at your teen's school for a referral.

Be assured that these disabilities do not mean that your teenager will never be able to perform in these areas. What they do mean is that your son or daughter needs extra help in dealing with these subjects. Expert teachers who understand these learning disorders can help your child learn in these subject areas.

A teenager who experiences a sudden drop in grades, but who has a history of

If you suspect your teen has a learning disability, the best way to find out is to have your child tested by a qualified school or clinical psychologist.

acceptable grades, probably is not evidencing a learning disability. That doesn't mean the sudden drop in grades should be ignored. Rather, the most likely cause is not a learning disability, but emotional problems or some kind of stressful situation. For more information about learning disabilities, you can contact:

The Coordinated Campaign for Learning Disabilities
888/478-6463
www.ldonline.org

Learning Disabilities Association of America
4156 Library Rd.
Pittsburgh, PA 15234
888/300-6710

National Center for Learning Disabilities
381 Park Ave. South, Suite 1401
New York, NY 10016
888/575-7373

Alcohol and Illegal Drug Use

among parents' worst fears is that their teenagers will develop alcohol or drug problems. And with good reason. In 1997, one in ten 12- to 17-year-olds reported using marijuana or hashish in the prior month. One in 20 reported having used some other illicit drug, including cocaine, crack, heroin, or LSD. By the time our teens become seniors in high school, half will have tried an illegal drug.

The picture is even worse when it comes to alcohol use. In 1997, one out of every five 12- to 17-year-olds reported having used alcohol in the previous month. Nearly one in ten reported having engaged in binge drinking. Overall, 80 percent of high school seniors report having used alcohol.

The scary part (if these statistics aren't scary enough) is that the average age of first initiation in the use of alcohol has declined to about 15.7 years old, compared to 17.4 years in 1987. Similar declines are being seen in first use of illicit drugs.

And the time between first initiation and the onset of problems is narrowing. In contrast, those who get through age 21 without using drugs or abusing alcohol are virtually certain never to do so.

The Worst Problem? Alcohol

Although most publicity is given to the detrimental and widespread use of illicit drugs, alcohol use exacts the greatest toll on our teens. Motor vehicle accidents, the majority of which involve alcohol use, kill more teenagers than does any other single cause of death. In fact, the most likely cause of death for a 16-year-old is alcohol related.

Compared to teens who don't drink alcohol, teens who do drink are more likely to:
• Have poor school performance
• Drop out of high school
• Experience depression
• Engage in early and promiscuous sexual activity
• Have troubled peer relationships

So don't be misled into believing that the use of alcohol or illicit drugs is only a reflection of adolescent angst. The danger is real.

Teens get involved with alcohol and illegal drugs use in a number of ways, but the biggest risk factors for adolescence substance abuse include:
• Running around in a peer group that drinks and does drugs
• Depression
• Older siblings who use alcohol and drugs and encourage their use
• Academic failure
• Poor parental monitoring
• Permissive parental attitudes about adolescents' use of alcohol and illicit drugs

Protecting Kids from Harm

The biggest protective factors against adolescent substance abuse include a warm and close relationship with one's parents, feeling connected to one's school, active

Helping Your Teen Say "No" to Drugs There are a number of things you can do to aid your teen in this difficult area. Here are some proven antidrug strategies from the National Center on Addiction and Substance Abuse (CASA) that you may not have thought of:

Eat meals as a family. Research shows that families who eat dinner together six or seven times a week have teens who are significantly less likely to get involved with drugs or alcohol.

Encourage attendance at religious services. Attending religious services four or more times a month has a strong deterrent effect on teen use of drugs and alcohol. According to Joseph A. Califano, chairman of CASA and former Secretary of the U.S. Department of Health and Human Services, religion "is a key factor in giving our children the moral values, skills, and will to say 'no' to illegal drugs, alcohol, and cigarettes."

▶

participation in religious activities, and a peer group that reinforces abstinence from drug and alcohol use.

In other words, those teens who feel connected to parents, school, faith, and nondeviant peer groups are the teens most likely to believe that alcohol and drug use during adolescence is unacceptable and begin drinking (if at all) at older ages. They are also the ones who are most resistant to peer pressure to use alcohol in social situations.

Youths' perceptions of the harmfulness of drugs and alcohol also affect their use

The way teens view the risk of alcohol and drug use is a strong determining factor of whether they'll actually use these substances.

of such substances. Unfortunately, less than half of youth ages 12 to 17 believe there is "great risk" in having five or more drinks once or twice a week.

Teens are also similarly misinformed about the risks involved in marijuana use and other illegal substances. This is unfortunate because research consistently shows that the way teens view the risk of alcohol and drug use is among the most important things that determine whether they'll actually use these substances.

Your Responsibility

What does this mean for you and your teen? To protect your teens from substance abuse, you need to do your job. And your job is to openly discuss with your teens your expectations and values concerning teenage drinking and the use of illicit drugs, and then monitor their behavior.

Unfortunately, too many parents are falling down on the job. According to a 1997 national survey of youth conducted by the Partnership for a Drug Free America, 85 percent of teens believe parents in general are doing a lot to prevent their child's drug use. At the same time, however, 54 percent of these same teenagers said they would like their own parents to do more.

Parents and teens perceive this difficulty as well. Whereas 94 percent of parents interviewed said they talked with their teens over the last year about drugs, only

◄ Have a parent at home after school. One of the highest-risk times for teen alcohol and drug use is after school, between the hours of 4 and 6 p.m. If both parents work outside the home, see if one can arrange a flexible work schedule so that the parent can be home during these critical after-school hours.

If neither parent can do this, arrange for another responsible adult to be at home. But don't rely on older siblings. If they are using drugs or alcohol themselves, their presence alone significantly increases the chances younger siblings will begin using alcohol and drugs as well.

Know your teen's whereabouts on weekends. Have your teen periodically check in by phoning home. Have your teen carry a pager with the understanding that you may page him or her at any time and expect a response to your page within 15 minutes.

67 percent of teens report discussions with their own parents about drugs.

In fact, according to a poll conducted by the Partnership for a Drug Free America, parents tend to underestimate the presence of drugs in the lives of their teens.

Although 59 percent of teens say they have been offered drugs, only 38 percent of parents believe that drugs have been offered to their teens. And whereas 71

> Although 59 percent of teens say they have been offered drugs, only 38 percent of parents believe that drugs have been offered to their teens.

percent of teens say they have friends who smoke marijuana, only 45 percent of parents believe their teens have friends who do.

"Babyboomer [parents] ... are surprisingly and ironically out of step with the reality of drugs in their children's lives," according to Richard D. Bonnette, president of the Partnership for a Drug Free America. When it comes to drugs and alcohol, it's likely that the conditions in the schools and on the streets are a whole lot worse than they were when you went to school.

Talk to Your Teen

So here's the deal about communication and drugs. When parents frequently and consistently express their expectations that teenagers should not use alcohol or illicit drugs, and have household rules against their use, their teens are less likely to become substance abusers.

When parents don't talk with their kids about alcohol and drugs, or, even worse, express permissive attitudes about their use, teens are much more likely to become substance abusers. Parents make the choice about what to say to their teens (if anything) about drugs and alcohol. Teens pay the price.

Here are some tips on how to talk to your kids about drugs and alcohol:

Talk early and often. The time to begin talking with your kids about the dangers of drugs and alcohol is not when they are teens, but when they are much younger. Don't be afraid to initiate conversations about the dangers of drugs and alcohol, using age-appropriate language, whenever the opportunity arises, such as during regular family mealtimes. If you have waited until your child is a teenager to talk about the dangers of drugs and alcohol, it's not too late. But do it now. Act as if your teen's life may depend upon it—because it does.

Give a consistent "no use" message. When kids have been given a consistent "no use" message throughout their childhoods, they are more likely to resist peer pressure to use drugs and alcohol when they are teens. Establish a clear "no use" family rule when it comes to illegal drug and alcohol use by teenagers, and stick with it. Make sure your

Resources for Talking To Kids About Drugs

The American Council for Drug Education
136 East 64th St.
New York, NY 10021
800/488-DRUG

"Just Say No" International
2101 Webster St., Suite 1300
Oakland, CA 94612
800/258-2766

National Clearinghouse on Alcohol and Drug Information
P.O. Box 2345
Rockville, MD 20847
800/729-6686

Partnership for a Drug Free America
405 Lexington Avenue
16th Floor
New York, NY 10174
212/922-1560

teen understands that you made these rules because you love him or her, not because you are a killjoy. Remember: Research shows that if your teen makes it to age 20 without ever having abused drugs or alcohol, he or she is virtually certain never to do so.

Give clear, accurate information. Give your teens accurate information about the dangers of drug and alcohol use. Explain to your younger teens what common illegal drugs look like, their street names, and how they can affect the body.

Don't be afraid to talk tough. Be sure your teens understand that some drugs, such as cocaine, crack, and inhalants, are very dangerous and can kill them even if they take them only once. Help your teen understand that drugs are not dangerous because they are illegal, they are illegal because they are dangerous.

Encourage questions and give honest answers. If you don't know something, admit it. Then go find out the answer and share it with your teen.

Don't just preach, listen. Teens feel more comfortable talking with their parents when they believe their parents genuinely want to hear what they have to say. This is especially important when it comes to sensitive issues, such as drug and alcohol use. By listening attentively to what your teen has to say and respecting your teen's feelings, you create an atmosphere in which your teen feels comfortable

Some Common Drugs Teens Abuse

Drug	Description	Common Name
Marijuana	Looks like dried leaves; smoked in a pipe or hand-rolled cigarette	Pot, weed, grass, herb, reefer, joints, roaches
Cocaine	Comes either in white powder (which is inhaled or "snorted") or a hardened paste (which is smoked in a pipe in a process called "free-basing")	Coke, snow, flake, blow, girl
Crack Cocaine	A solid nugget smoked in a pipe	Crack, freebase rocks, rock
LSD	A manufactured hallucinogenic in tablet, capsule, or occasionally liquid form. Often added to absorbent paper, such as blotter paper, and divided into small decorative squares with each square representing one dose	Acid, green/red dragon
MDMA	A manufactured hallucinogenic in pill or powder form, taken orally or injected	Ecstasy, Adam, STP, XTC
PCP	A white crystalline powder easily mixed with dyes to make tablets, capsules, and colored powders	Angel dust, ozone, wack, loveboat, boat
Mescaline, Psilocybin, Peyote	Hallucinogenic mushrooms	Magic mushrooms, buttons, cactus, shrooms
Amphetamine	Pill, or, occasionally, powder, form	Speed, black beauties, crosses, hearts
Methamphetamine	A powerful form of amphetamine that comes in clear chunky crystals (called glass, chalk, ice) or powder (called crank)	Ice, crank, meth, crystal, glass, chalk
Methaqualone	A powerful depressant in pill form	Quaalude, ludes

coming to you when he or she has a problem or question.

Provide help to them with saying "no." One of the hardest things for a teen to do is to stand up to peer pressure to conform. Yet, peer pressure is the most important reason why teens experiment with drugs and alcohol. Let your teen know you understand the need for peer group acceptance, and help him or her develop strategies for politely turning down offers to use drugs and alcohol.

Help them understand what makes a good friend. You can't choose friends for your teens, but you can help them understand what makes a good friend. Help your teens understand that a good friend is someone who shares their values, respects their decisions, and listens to their feelings, and that anyone who would pressure them to drink or take drugs isn't really a friend at all.

Help them feel good about themselves. Low self-esteem and depression are two important reasons why teens turn to illegal drugs and alcohol use. When parents are encouraging and reward positive behavior, teens are much less likely to seek comfort through drugs and alcohol.

Encourage positive peer group activities. Teens who are involved in enjoyable and worthwhile activities, such as after-school clubs, religious programs, and sports, are more likely to make friends and develop interests that will help keep them away from drugs and alcohol.

Be a good role model. If you use illegal drugs yourself or drive while under the influence of alcohol, expect your teens to do so as well. If you want your teens to

inhalants: sniffing fumes

When most parents think of drug abuse problems, cocaine, marijuana, and LSD frequently come to mind. But there is another substance that teenagers sometimes abuse that can be just as dangerous: inhalants.

Inhalants are mostly legal products that can cause someone to experience a high by sniffing its fumes. (Kids sometimes call this "huffing.") There are over 1,000 different products that can be abused in this way, including many commonly found in the home, the office, or at school. These include glues, gasoline, spray paints, polishes, aerosol sprays, nail polish remover, typewriter fluid, even room deodorizers.

Younger adolescents are the most at risk of inhalant abuse. The American Academy of Pediatrics estimates that as many as 20 percent of eighth graders have tried some form of an inhalant. Adolescents and pre-teens are attracted to inhalants because they are relatively easy to use, are easy to obtain and to hide, and are legal to possess.

Unfortunately, teens and parents are often unaware of the dangers associated with the use of inhalants. The truth is that inhalants can cause a variety of problems, including permanent brain damage and death. Most frighteningly, teens can die from inhalants the very first time they use them or any time thereafter.

Symptoms that a teen is abusing inhalants include breath and clothing that smell like chemicals, spots or sores around the mouth, unexplained paint or other stains on their clothing, and appearing drunk or dazed. Inhalants are so dangerous that if you suspect your teen of abusing them, you should seek treatment immediately.

understand that "no use" of illegal drugs is best, you will have to set the example. And if you do drink alcohol, do so responsibly. Setting a good example is one of the most important things you can do as a parent.

If you suspect a problem, seek help. There are several signs that indicate that there may be a problem:

- Becoming withdrawn
- Hanging out with a questionable group of friends
- Weight loss
- Poor performance in school
- Extreme moodiness
- Frequent arguments
- Unexplained violent outbursts
- Glassy eyes

If you see any of these signs, or have other reasons to suspect that your teen may be abusing alcohol or illegal drugs, you'll need help dealing with the problem. A good place to start is talking with your teen's pediatrician, who will know good referral sources for help in your community.

Allergies and Asthma

Sneezing, sniffling, runny eyes ... No, it's not a cold; it's just that time of year again.

A teen with an allergy has abnormal responses to a normal substance—something, say, like peanuts or pollen. That substance, called an allergen, revs up the immune system in much the same way that a virus would. The result is inflammation, irritation, and discomfort. Most allergies fall into one of two categories—respiratory allergies or food allergies.

Respiratory Allergies

Hay fever is one example of a respiratory allergy. People who have this problem suffer with red, runny eyes, a runny nose, sneezing, and/or a wheezy chest when exposed to pollens. Others have the same response to household dust or household pets.

Here are some suggestions to reduce the number of allergy attacks your teen experiences.

Fight the mite. The major culprit indoors is the common dust mite. These tiny members of the spider family thrive indoors, where the environment is warm and humid.

Actually, it's not the mite itself that causes trouble, it is the microscopic mite's even more microscopic droppings.

To make your teen's room less attractive to mites:

Get Help Fast If...

Your teen may need emergency help for asthma if he or she:

- Is so short of breath that he or she cannot speak a complete sentence
- Has trouble breathing when lying down
- Relies on neck or stomach muscles to breathe
- Becomes sleepy as breathing worsens
- Makes no wheezing sound while experiencing extreme shortness of breath

- Get rid of any wall-to-wall carpeting.
- Use short-pile throw rugs, and launder them once a week.
- Reduce the humidity in the room to below 50 percent by plugging in an air conditioner or dehumidifier.
- Avoid feather pillows, down comforters, quilts, wool blankets, and other bed linens that are not easily laundered in HOT (130-degree) water.
- Wash bed linens every week.
- Wash curtains every two weeks in 130-degree water.
- Lock out mites and their messes by sealing your teen's mattress and pillow in plastic cases.

Ban the dander. Another source of year-round allergy is animal dander (scales shed from an animal's skin or hair, or from a bird's feathers). Your little lap cat will have to move outdoors or find a new home. Puppy dog, too. If you simply can't part with your pet, at least keep it out of your teen's room and shampoo and brush it often.

Declare your home a smoke-free zone. Tell all your friends who smoke that they will have to step outside if they want to light up.

Shut out pollen. Trees release pollen in spring, grasses release it in summer, and ragweed spews it into the air in late summer and early fall. The pollen count is usually highest in the early morning and begins to drop off by noon. Tell your teen to close the windows at bedtime so pollen doesn't drift into the room on sunrise breezes.

Put a hold on mold. Fight mildew and molds with hot, soapy water, with chlorine bleach, or with special products sold to kill mold.

Food Allergies

If your teenager was allergic to certain foods as a baby, chances are that he or she has grown out of it. Most kids do, usually by the age of 6. But some people experience problems with foods all their lives.

The most common offenders are cow's milk; eggs; corn; citrus fruit; nuts; peanuts; chocolate; seafood; and wheat, barley, or rye gluten.

Signs of a food allergy include:
- Abdominal pain
- Diarrhea, and/or vomiting
- Fainting
- Hives
- Swollen lips, tongue, throat, eyes, and face
- Asthma

The best treatment for food allergies is avoidance. Sometimes, however, avoidance is impossible. Your doctor will be able to suggest or prescribe medications that keep allergic reactions under control.

Resources for Allergy Relief

The Johns Hopkins University Dermatology, Allergy, and Immunology (DACI) Reference Laboratory will assess the allergens in your air, testing for one of the following: mold spore count, dust mite (Der p), cat, dust mite (Der f), or cockroach. The first test costs about $36, with additional tests $25 each. Call 800/882-4110 for information.

The Environmental Protection Agency in Washington, DC, will send you a list of recommended air filtering devices. Call 800/222-LUNG.

Allergy Publications, Box 640, Menlo Park, CA 94026 will send a free listing of products and services compiled by the American Allergy Association.

To find a specialist, call the **American Academy of Allergy & Immunology** at 800/822-ASMA

allergy hotline and networks

The following sources of helpful information are recommended by the **National Institute of Allergy and Infectious Diseases:**

Hotline: Immunologic Diseases, sponsored by the National Jewish Hospital in Denver. Nurses are available to answer questions. 800/222-LUNG.

Food Allergy Network: Guidelines for Patients, Parents, and Teachers, 4744 Holly Ave. Fairfax VA 22030. 703/691-3179.

Allergy and Asthma Network/Mothers of Asthmatics, Inc., 3554 Chain Bridge Rd. Ste. 2000, Fairfax VA 22030. 800/878-4403.

American Lung Association, 1740 Broadway, New York, NY 10019-4374. 800/LUNG-USA.

Parents of Asthmatic/Allergic Children, 1412 Marathon Dr., Ft. Collins CO 80524. 303/842-7395.

Asthma

Asthma is the most common chronic lung disease of adolescence. It is caused when muscle spasms constrict the flow of air to the lungs. The linings of the airways become inflamed and swollen, and excess mucus may clog the airways.

Anyone having an asthma attack has labored or restricted breathing, a tight feeling in the chest, coughing, and—characteristically—wheezing. As people with asthmatic airways breathe in, they open up their chests and the airways within grow bigger. As a result, air can move past accumulated mucus. But, when they try to breathe out, the airways become smaller again. Mucus obstructs them, trapping air in the lungs.

Asthma can develop quickly and can range from mild discomfort to life-threatening attacks in which breathing stops altogether. Its most common cause is allergy.

Responding to an Asthma Attack

Kids with asthma learn early how to use an inhaler, a handheld device that delivers a bronchodilator—a type of medicine that opens up the airways. One or two puffs usually quiets an attack. The inhaler should not be used more frequently than four times a day. If your teenager feels the need to use them more often, you should discuss it with your doctor. The most commonly prescribed bronchodilators are Ventolin, Proventil, and Alupent.

Other medications also can be dispensed from an inhaler, including cromolyn sodium and corticosteroids. Both help to control overall inflammation in the airways, but don't stop an asthma attack.

Doctors also may prescribe oral prednisone, a corticosteroid, that puts the brakes on asthma. Because this drug is very powerful and can have serious side effects (interference with growth, susceptibility to infection, and more), it is prescribed so that the doses become smaller and smaller. The goal is to discontinue the drug without provoking an allergy attack.

Blame Those Genes:

If either you or your spouse suffers from allergies, your son or daughter is twice as likely as others to inherit an allergic condition. If you both have allergies, your kid's risk increases about four times.

Body Piercing, Tattooing, and Branding

gary had his tongue pierced one Saturday morning. As instructed, he filled his mouth with ice chips to keep the swelling down. He went to a party that night, just waiting to show off his new stud. He arrived dribbling melted ice tinged with pink from a little residual bleeding. "Eeew, Gary, you're gross," said his girlfriend … "Go away!" At home, his parents were looking up the number of a psychologist.

Piercing. In case you haven't noticed, it's everywhere. A 1997 Miss America contestant wore a navel ring in the bathing suit competition. Scary Spice, one of the Spice Girls, sticks out her studded tongue at the audience. Kids see body piercing as glamorous, sexy, and exciting. They need to be saved from themselves.

The major piercing fads among teens are multiple holes in the ear, multiple rings in the eyebrow, navel rings, and tongue studs.

"Why do kids do it?" Sloan Beth Karver, M.D., wonders aloud. "When I encounter a teen with something like a tongue stud, I make a point of not mentioning it. I don't want to cater to that particular cry for attention. I'll provide attention in other ways."

Good Reasons to Say No

Kids who get pierced, indeed, are seeking to distinguish themselves from the rest of the crowd. They do want extra attention. As a parent, you might want to investigate less permanent and damaging ways to allow your teen to stand apart— temporarily—from the rest.

Dr. Karver notes that each of these piercings shares a common problem—infection. Have your teen recite the following ditty: "Any hole in the skin lets germs in."

The major piercing fads among teens are multiple holes in the ear, multiple rings in the eyebrow, navel rings, and tongue studs.

In addition, each piercing has its own individual problem. With multiple holes in the ear, there is danger of cartilage collapse. Navel rings are irritated by belts and waistbands. In fact, they can be pulled hard enough to tear the flesh. Tongue studs make people talk funny, and look funny, too.

Kids who are into piercing say that it's addictive. If one earring is neat, 12 earrings are fabulous! And how about piercing the webbed flesh between each finger? Or getting a nose stud?

So discourage your teen from getting his or her body pierced for as long as possible—hopefully forever. The urge simply may pass. If not, you may at least have prevented some serial piercings. Above all, you must absolutely forbid home piercing. Using a sewing needle is dangerous and unsanitary, and the results may not be what your teen expected.

As with tattooing, body piercing may or may not be regulated in your city or state. You will have to call your local Department of Health to get the lowdown on your area.

Tattoos Are Forever

Zoe and Ted are smart, athletic, good-looking teenagers. He's on the high school football team, and she's a cheerleader. Everyone considers them a "wholesome" dating couple.

After one Saturday's big winning game over an arch-rival, the team, the band, and the cheerleaders went from the high school into town to celebrate.

When Zoe returned home, she announced to her parents, "I got a tattoo. Almost all the kids are getting one!"

"Oh, Zoe! What an absolutely dumb thing to do," her mother wailed. "You'll be stuck with that thing for your whole life."

"People will think you're some kind of 'biker babe,'" said her father. "What were you thinking?"

Zoe's parents settled down a little when they saw the tattoo. She displayed a tiny ladybug on her big toe. They are not pleased, but they are relieved that it's not

selecting a safe studio

f your teen is dead set on getting that tattoo, and you don't think you can stop it, then make sure he or she reads this information. (Please understand. We're not advocating tattoos, just trying to prevent serious infection in youngsters who think they need to do this to themselves.)

The only thing between you and all the rest of the dirty old world is your skin. When you stick needles in it, pierce it, or burn it, you make holes in it that allow infection and disease to get in. Therefore, it's extremely important to select your artist and body art studio knowledgeably.

Carl Hesse, a professional tattooist in Perksie, Pennsylvania, since 1979, offers the following tips.

- Look for a studio that is clean and well kept.
- Ask if the artist is a member of the National Tattoo Association or the Alliance of Professional Tattooists, or has completed a seminar in preventing disease transmission.
- Ask to see the autoclave sterilizer. This machine uses heat, steam, and pressure at temperatures above 270° F to kill germs and other microorganisms. (If there is no such machine on the premises, you're in the wrong place.)
- Ask to see the autoclave monthly monitoring certificate, showing that it passed its monthly tests.
- Make sure the materials used in the application of your tattoo are "single service." That is, each needle and tube set is individually packaged, dated, and sealed, then autoclaved.
- Examine the bag containing the sets. It should bear an icon that has changed color (it usually turns black) when properly sterilized.
- Ask the artist to disinfect all work surfaces and surrounding space with a germ-killing cleaner both before and after application of your tattoo.
- Be sure the artist is wearing disposable latex gloves.
- Make sure the artist disposes of used needles in a "sharps" container—never directly in a waste basket.

something like a dagger on her forearm, or a lurid red rose on her breast.

Ted also got a tattoo. He now sports his team number—in school colors—on his right shoulder blade. His father, who bears the legend "Semper Fi" on his bulging bicep, is actually a little pleased. Ted's mom is just glad the tattoo is no bigger than a half-dollar.

Tattoos: Youthful Acceptance

What's happening here? Tattoos used to be the province of bikers and drunken sailors on shore leave. Today, however, even some "nice" girls and boys like Zoe and Ted are getting tattoos. Or getting their bodies pierced—and not just their earlobes, either! And now one of the latest fads among college students is branding.

What's going on, say the practitioners of "body art" as they call it, is that the social taboo against the tattoo has greatly diminished in the last decade. Tattoos have become fashion statements. Butterflies, roses, four-leaf clovers, and rainbows have joined—maybe even replaced—the bawdy hula dancer, the skull and crossbones, and the coiled cobra. Young women today are as likely as young men to buy the designs offered in a tattoo studio, say tattoo artists.

Zoe and Ted are pretty lucky, because they may—just—be able to live with their tattoos for the rest of their lives. But how about those kids of yesteryear who, as forty-somethings, now have to appear in public with little blue Smurfs on their arms? (But they seemed so cute back in 1982!)

Discouraging the Deed

Unfortunately, you can't always depend upon the law to help you keep your child out of a tattoo parlor. Some cities, such as New York, have banned the practice of tattooing altogether. Some states have, too. But in several states (Maryland, Idaho, Michigan, and a few others) tattooing is unregulated.

In many other states, minors may not be tattooed without parental consent—which is frequently forged. A complete list of state legislation is impossible because it is in flux. As the practice of tattooing grows, many states that had no regulations before are beginning to sit up and take notice. For information about tattoo regulation where you live, call your local Department of Health.

If you want to keep your kids out of the tattoo parlor, talk to them straight. Tell them that:

• There's a good chance they will choose a design that later will embarrass them, or that they will grow tired of.
• It's wise to wait a few months to be sure they still want a) a tattoo, and b) that particular design.
• Tattoo removal is expensive and out of the reach of most people.
• The results of tattoo removal are highly variable.
• There is a danger of Hepatitis B and other infections.

Body Branding

A branding is done with a white hot piece of metal that etches a design into the flesh. The result is a third-degree burn. That's the worst kind of burn, the kind that should be treated by a doctor. Eventually a scab forms. When the scab falls off, the skin shows the design as a raised, smooth scar.

Here are some facts to pass on to your teen:

- Third degree burns are highly susceptible to infection, especially if the scab cracks. And they usually do.
- Third degree burns hurt a lot.
- Third degree burns can take quite a long time to heal.

Also tell your teen that the branding artist cannot guarantee the results of the process. He or she does not create the brand, the body does. And each body makes scars differently. Some brandings look black, others look pink. Some are smooth, while others have a ropy surface.

In other words, what you see in the design catalog is not necessarily what you get.

Dating and Sexuality

It's easy to get the impression in today's highly sexualized culture that every teenager in America is having sex.

Don't believe it. The reality is most teenagers in high school are not having sexual intercourse. According to the most recent data available from the U.S. Centers for Disease Control some 49 percent of high school boys and 48 percent of high school girls have had sexual intercourse. This means that high school students who are not sexually experienced are actually in the majority.

It's also easy to get the impression that there is little, if anything, anyone—and especially parents—can do to stop teenagers from having sex. Don't believe that either. The percentage of sexually active teens aged 15 to 19 has actually decreased by 11 percent since 1991. Somebody must be doing something right.

And thank goodness. The fact is teens who engage in early sexual intercourse are more likely to do poorly at school, use alcohol and illicit drugs, and smoke cigarettes than those who don't. Sexually active teenagers also have the highest rate of sexually transmitted diseases of any age group.

Too Soon for Sex

And, of course, there is the risk of teenage pregnancy. Each year, one in 10 girls under the age of 20—one million every year—becomes pregnant. Forty percent of these pregnancies will end in abortion, 10 percent in miscarriage, and 50 percent in live births. Becoming a teen mom makes it less likely that the girl will ever finish high school, get a good job, and

Good Resources for More Information:

Institute for Youth Development
P.O. Box 16560
Washington, DC 20041
703/471-8750

National Abstinence Clearinghouse
801 East 41st St.
Sioux Falls, SD 57105
888/577-2966
e-mail: takecharge@alpha-center.org

National Campaign to Prevent Teen Pregnancy
2100 M Street, NW, Suite 300
Washington, DC 20037

get married or, if she does get married, stay married. Becoming a teen dad can be just as devastating to a boy's future.

But even if teenagers were able to avoid sexually transmitted diseases or teenage pregnancy, it still wouldn't be a good idea for them to be having sex. Sex is a wonderful and marvelous activity, provided it is engaged in within its proper context. Two 14-year-olds having sex in the back seat of a car is hardly the proper context.

Teenage sexual activity brings with it the potential for tremendous heartbreak. Teens are simply not mature enough to handle the intense emotions that go along with sexual activity—no matter how "in love" they profess to be.

Besides, what parents want most for their teens is not simply to avoid the negative consequences associated with high-risk behaviors, like early sexual activity, but to lead a fulfilling and enriching life. As Karen Pittman, senior vice president of the International Youth Foundation, has put it, "What parent on earth wants to say, 'I am so proud of my kid. You know, she's 15, and hasn't gotten pregnant and hasn't stabbed anyone. My 15-year-old son hasn't been in jail yet, and he wears a condom.'"

You Have to Talk

So what's a parent to do? Research consistently indicates that parents who are successful in helping their teens refrain from sexual activity do two things: They talk to their kids about sex, and they monitor their teens' behavior.

Unfortunately, many parents are reluctant to talk with their teens about sex.

rules for dating

a parent's first line of defense against teenage sex is setting the rules for dating. Here are some commonsense suggestions:

Insist on a slow start. Do what you can to discourage early, frequent, and steady dating at least until age 16. Early, frequent, and steady dating is one of the single biggest risk factors for teenage sexual activity. Hold the line.

Establish dating rules and expectations. Establish rules early on for such things as curfews and dating activities—before your teen starts coming up with his or her own plans.

Teach your teen to date responsibly. Encourage your teenager to avoid sexually stimulating TV shows, videos, and movies when dating. Teach your daughters to reject boys' lines, such as, "If you really love me, you'll do this for me," or "You know we both want to, so don't act like such a prude." And teach your sons not to say such things.

Don't allow your teens to date older persons. Teenage girls tend to have their first sexual experience with male partners who are three or more years older. For teenage boys, their first sexual encounter is likely to be with girls who are less than a year older. Be smart. Only allow your teenager to date persons of the same age.

Have them date in groups. Encourage your teenager to hang out in groups. When dating, encourage your teen to date with a buddy or friend. They can help each other out of difficult or tempting situations.

Always meet and greet. Insist that you meet the person dating your son or daughter each time before they go out. This will establish the message that you are watching.

According to researcher Marcela Raffaelli, Ph. D., assistant professor of psychology, and her colleagues at the University of Nebraska at Lincoln, nearly half of teens report never having had even one good talk with their mothers about any sexual topic. Seventy percent said they had never had a good talk with their fathers about sex.

Yet most teens actually want their parents to talk to them about sex. According to a 1997 survey by the Henry J. Kaiser Foundation, when asked who they would be most likely to ask to get information about how to prevent pregnancy, 71 percent of 13- to 15-year-olds said their parents. Sixty-three percent said they would be most likely to ask a parent about the basic facts of sexual reproduction, and 60 percent said they would be most likely to ask a parent about issues related to relationships and becoming sexually active.

What do teens want to know? According to a 1998 poll conducted by the National Campaign to Prevent Teen Pregnancy, 22 percent said the one thing they would most like to discuss with their parents was knowing how and when to say "no." Twenty-one percent said they would like to know more about managing dating relationships. Another poll found that 58 percent of 10- to 12-year-olds want help from their parents in dealing with pressure to have sex.

Here's the lesson: If you want your teenagers to refrain from engaging in sex, you're going to have to overcome your own embarassment and talk with them about it. And not just about the mechanics of sex, but also about your values and expectations about their behavior. Most especially, don't be afraid to talk to your teen about abstinence.

You Have to Set Standards

What teens are really yearning for is not so much sex, but love. A 1997 *Parade* magazine poll, for example, found that after happiness and longevity, what teens want most out of life is to be married and have a family. In a survey conducted by the Kaiser Family Foundation and *YM* magazine, 87 percent of girls and 62 percent of boys thought saving sex for later in life is a "good thing." In fact, according to the National Longitudinal Study on Adolescent Health—a national study of nearly 100,000 adolescents in grades 7 through 12, fully 16 percent of adolescent girls and 10 percent of adolescent boys had signed a written pledge of virginity until marriage.

Yet despite this yearning on the part of teenagers for help

The Word on Sex

It's no secret that too many teens are having sex before they're emotionally ready to handle the consequences. If you're concerned about protecting your teens, you're not alone. Here's a quick look at what parents need to know. You'll see that the role that parents play in a teen's sexual life is extremely important.

Risk factors for sexual involvement:

- Parents who are less emotionally supportive
- Permissive parental attitudes regarding teen sexual behavior
- Low levels of parental monitoring
- Paid work outside the home of more than 19 hours per week
- Appearing older than other teens of the same age
- Teen's use of alcohol, illicit drugs, and cigarettes
- Poor school performance
- Involvement in a steady, ongoing dating relationship
- Low religiosity

Protective factors:

- Teens who feel connected to their families and school
- Close parental monitoring of teen behavior
- Having parents that disapprove of the use of contraceptives (for unmarried teens)
- Participation in religious activities
- Taking a pledge of virginity
- Appearing younger than other teens of the same age

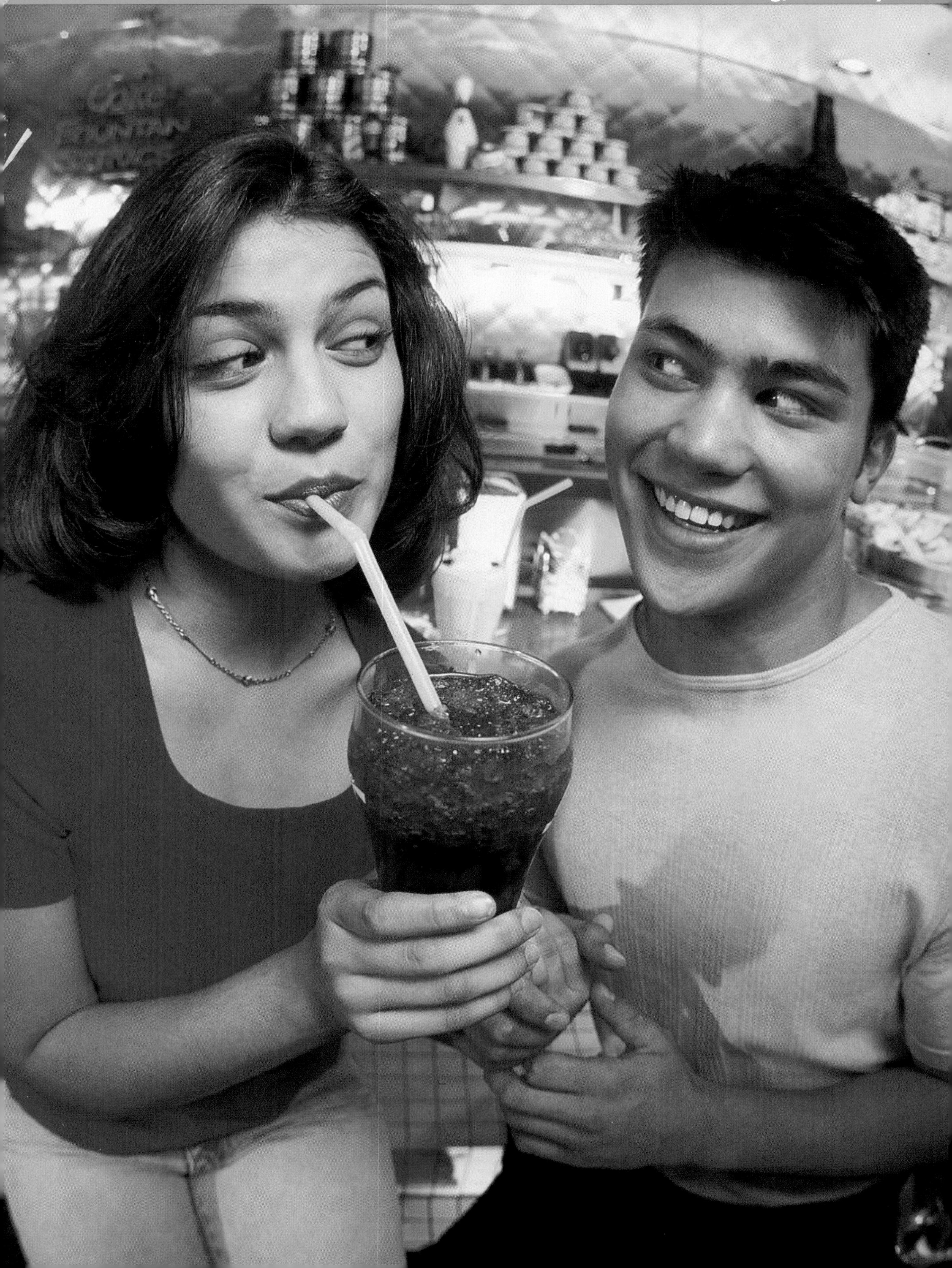

sexually transmitted diseases

Of the 12 million cases of sexually transmitted diseases (STDs) that occur each year, 3 million (or 25 percent) are among teenagers. About 13 percent of youth ages 13 to 19 contract an STD each year. The most common STDs are:

Chlamydia. This most common bacterial STD is found in 20 to 40 percent of teens having sex outside of marriage. Up to 40 percent of all girls between the ages of 15 and 19 are infected—the highest chlamydia infection rate of any age group. Chlamydia often has no overt symptoms, and if untreated can cause sterility in both males and females.

Human Papilloma Virus (HPV). Up to 15 percent of sexually active teenage girls are infected with HPV. The majority of those infected have a strain that has been linked to cervical cancer.

Genital Warts. Viral growths that appear on the external genital organs, genital warts infect as many as a third of all sexually active teenagers. No permanent cure exists for these growths, with at least 20 percent recurring following removal. In females, there is an association between genital warts and cervical cancer.

> **Up to 15 percent of sexually active girls are infected with the Human Papilloma Virus (HPV).**

Herpes. This is a viral infection that, undiagnosed, can cause miscarriage or stillbirth during pregnancy. There is no cure.

Gonorrhea. A highly contagious bacterial infection affecting the penis in men and the vagina in women, gonorrhea, left untreated, can cause sterility, arthritis, and heart trouble.

Syphilis. A serious, highly contagious, progressive bacterial disease that can affect all parts of the body—the brain, bones, spinal cord, heart, and reproductive organs. New cases of syphilis in the U.S. fell during 1996 to their lowest level in 40 years—4.4 cases per 100,000. This is close to the historic low of 3.9 cases per 100,000 that occurred in 1956 and 1957.

AIDS. Acquired immune deficiency syndrome (AIDS) is a disease in which the body's natural defense system is disabled, allowing other bacterial and viral infections to become deadly. As of June 1997, the National Centers for Disease Control had counted 2,953 cases among adolescents aged 13 to 19, representing less than 1 percent of the total number of AIDS cases in the U.S.

Since the time between infection with HIV and the onset of AIDS may be several years, however,

Dad, there's a rumor going around the high school that this guy is HIV positive. I don't believe it though. Kids my age don't get AIDS, we're too young. Besides, no one else in the school has AIDS, where could he have gotten it?

I wouldn't be so sure what you heard isn't true. Kids your age DO get AIDS, and AIDS is fatal. AIDS may not show up for several years, so it's possible that others at your school DO have it and don't know it yet.

many young adults diagnosed with AIDS undoubtedly contracted the disease while teenagers. In fact, half of all HIV infections in the U.S. occur among persons under 25. There is as yet no cure for AIDS. Although new drugs are increasing the survival time for people who get AIDS and researchers are making progress in understanding it, the disease is still ultimately fatal.

in postponing sexual activity, one out of five parents say it would be all right with them for their teenager to have sex once or twice with a steady boyfriend or girlfriend. One out of ten said they would not discourage their child from having sex. It is simply horrifying that so many parents are apparently willing to abdicate their responsibility to protect their teenagers from an activity that is known to present such high risks for negative outcomes.

Nor does being "nonjudgmental" help. When it comes to teenage sex, simply telling our kids to "follow their own conscience" and to "make good choices" doesn't work.

Teens need us to set high standards and expectations for appropriate behavior. This isn't just our opinion. According to the National Longitudinal Study of Adolescent Health, the largest study of its kind ever undertaken, one of the best protective factors against teen sex and pregnancy were parents who communicated a clear message of disapproval of teen sex and contraceptive use.

But talking isn't enough. You're also going to have to monitor their behavior.

In a 1998 poll, 22 percent of teens said the one thing they would most like to discuss with their parents was knowing how and when to say "no."

"Trust but verify" helped win the Cold War. It can also help win the war against teen pregnancy.

Get to know who your teen's friends are, what your teenager likes to read, listen to, and watch, and know what your teen is doing after school as well as on weekends and at night. Keep in mind that among the most likely times for teenagers to engage in sex is between the hours of 4 and 6 p.m.—after school when no parents are at home. Another high-risk activity is unsupervised parties, where teens can be tempted to pair up and go into separate bedrooms. So be sure the parties your teen goes to are adult supervised.

Still, by far the best prevention of all is for parents to be positively involved with and connected to their children's lives. Having a good relationship with one's parents is what motivates teenagers to obey household rules and incorporate their parents' values as their own. Nowhere is this more important than in the area of teenage sexual behavior.

What to Do if Your Teen Is Sexually Active

Sometimes, despite a parent's best efforts to the contrary, teenagers do become sexually active. Many parents, upon discovering their teen is sexually active, react with anger and rejection. Doing so is not going to help matters. Rather than recriminations, what sexually active teens need is help in thinking through their options.

The first thing a parent needs to help their sexually active teen think about is safety. This means encouraging teens who are sexually active to take precautions to prevent both pregnancy and sexually transmitted diseases (STDs).

The most effective means for preventing pregnancy are oral contraceptives or birth control pills. A female taking oral contraceptives—which are available by prescription only—has less than a 1 percent chance of getting pregnant. But to be effective, oral contraceptives must be taken daily. Herein lies one problem. Teenagers are notoriously forgetful. Forgetting to take oral contraceptives regularly can render them ineffective in preventing pregnancy. Another limitation of oral contraceptives is that they do nothing to prevent the transmission of STDs.

One "over the counter" method for preventing pregnancy is the latex condom. To be effective, latex condoms must be used correctly. Unfortunately, teenagers are often embarrassed or reluctant to use condoms. Even when used correctly, condoms are only 70 to 90 percent effective at preventing pregnancy and the transmission of STDs. Teens need to know that while condoms reduce the possibility of pregnancy and of catching an STD, condoms do not eliminate the risk entirely. As such, they make sex safer, not 100 percent safe.

Other means of contraception include hormonal implants, intrauterine devices (IUDs), spermicides, contraceptive sponges, diaphragms, and cervical caps. Each has its advantages and disadvantages. While it is important to talk to sexually active teens about these alternatives, they need to know that none of these methods protects 100 percent against both pregnancy and STDs. And, certainly, none protects against the emotional heartache that can result from a relationship breaking up following sexual intimacy.

One other option to discuss with a sexually active teen is "secondary virginity." Often, we act as if once a teen becomes sexually active, there is no way that teen can ever hope to restrain himself or herself from sexual activity in the future. This is not so. There are many examples of teens (and even unmarried adults) who have recommitted themselves successfully to sexual abstinence after having been sexually active. Given that no contraceptive is 100 percent effective in preventing both pregnancy and STDs, parents of sexually active teens should encourage their teen to consider this option as well.

Depression

although most teens describe themselves as usually happy, more adolescents today experience symptoms of serious depression than any generation in modern history.

According to the National Institute of Mental Health, as many as 1.5 million children and adolescents—2.5 percent of all children under the age of 18—suffer from serious depression. The American Academy of Child and Adolescent Psychiatry puts the number even higher, at 3.4 million. More than half a million teens between the ages of 13 and 17 are currently being prescribed an anti-depressant. Any way you look at it, that's a lot of depressed kids.

Of course, everyone gets "blue" once in a while. And, let's face it, moodiness can be a common feature of adolescence. What distinguishes normal, occasional sadness from depression is its severity and duration.

Serious depression is characterized by episodes of persistent depressed moods that last at least two weeks, generally accompanied by a loss of interest or pleasure in usual activities. The average duration of episodes of major depression is about 7 months.

Symptoms of adolescent depression include:

- crying a lot
- frequent nightmares
- not having fun anymore
- not wanting to spend time with peers
- feelings of hopelessness and worthlessness
- loss of appetite
- weight changes
- decreased energy
- difficulty thinking or concentrating
- feeling no one loves them
- being angry all the time at one's parents
- feeling lonely
- self-hatred

You should not try to deal with your teenager's extended bouts of depression by yourself. If the depression seems to go beyond the blues— even if you're not sure whether it's serious or not—it's important to make an appointment with a doctor for evaluation and possible treatment.

How Serious Is Depression?

The most serious symptoms of major depression are suicidal thoughts and attempts at suicide. Suicidal thoughts should never be taken lightly and are especially dangerous if accompanied by a plan. Tragically, suicide rates for children and teens have quadrupled since 1950. Each year, more than half a million youth in the U.S. attempt suicide. Of these, more than 2,000 succeed.

Serious depression is more common in girls than boys largely because girls tend to dwell on their problems more than boys do. They also worry more about things they can't control easily, such as personal appearance, peer popularity, and family problems.

Although prior to adolescence, depression rates are similar for boys and girls, beginning at about age 11, the rate at which girls experience depression increases significantly. By 18 years of age, girls are about twice as likely to experience depression. Girls also tend to stay depressed

Risk Factors for Teenage Depression

- divorce and other family problems
- controlling, rejecting, guilt-inducing, or uninterested parents
- social inadequacy or withdrawal
- anxiety
- shyness
- tendency to blame oneself for failures and to misread neutral scenarios as rejection
- history of depression in other family members

Signs Your Teen May Be Experiencing Serious Depression

- sudden changes in grades or loss of interest in usual activities
- sustained periods of sadness not related to a pecific event, such as family divorce or a breakup with a romantic partner
- increasing social isolation
- talk about suicide or obsession with death
- beginning to give away treasured personal items

longer than boys do. But this doesn't mean that teenage boys don't experience serious depression. In fact, while females attempt suicide 3 to 10 times more often than males, males succeed 5 times more often than females.

Despite its seriousness, depression often gets less attention in adolescence than in adulthood because depressed teens are often less disruptive than teens with conduct problems and because adults too frequently dismiss teen depression as moodiness. But the consequences of teen depression can be serious, including

Serious depression is more common in girls than boys largely because girls tend to dwell on their problems more than boys do.

adversely affected family and peer relationships, poor school performance, substance abuse, and suicide.

Treating Depression

Treatment for depression usually involves some combination of medication and therapy. The most common medications for treating depression in adolescence are Prozac, Zoloft, and Paxil. Be aware that these medications can have potentially harmful side effects, and so should only be taken under the careful supervision of a physician.

The most effective psychological interventions are skills-based approaches that help adolescents change the way they approach, interpret, and manage problems. Therapeutic approaches that simply focus on problems by talking about them may only serve to intensify, rather than decrease, depression. Where suicidal thoughts or attempts are present, psychiatric hospitalization is often warranted.

The best "treatment" for adolescent depression is prevention. Teens whose parents are accepting, affectionate, and willing to listen with care to their teens, and who cultivate and praise their teens' strengths, are significantly less likely to experience serious depression.

Other factors that have been found to lessen the risk of depression for adolescents are parental optimism toward the future and regular attendance at religious services. In fact, one study by psychologist Lisa Miller, Ph.D., assistant professor of psychology and education at Columbia University in New York City, found that young women reared in homes with a devoutly religious mother were 50 percent less likely to experience depression than other young women. And if the daughter grew up to share her mother's religious denomination, the risk of depression fell an additional 30 percent.

So the most important things parents can do to ensure that teenagers' occasional moodiness doesn't escalate into full-blown depression are to spend time with them showing that they care about them, express optimism toward the future, and encourage regular attendance at religious activities.

Eating Disorders

Weigh each morsel of food on a kitchen scale. Count each green pea on the plate. Today eat no more than four of them. Sneak into the bedroom closet to wolf down a hidden cache of candy bars, chips, and a bag of cookies. Stare into the mirror at eyes made red from the strain of vomiting.

This is the world of a teenager with an eating disorder.

Anorexia nervosa and bulimia nervosa are eating disorders that affect mostly adolescent girls and young women. The National Institute of Mental Health (NIMH) reports that about 1 percent of adolescent girls develop anorexia, and 2 to 3 percent develop bulimia. These diseases usually start about the time of puberty or in the early teen years. It's important to note that while it's mostly girls who get eating disorders, it is possible for boys to get them, too.

The consequences of eating disorders can be severe. The NIMH says that 1 in 10 cases leads to death from starvation, cardiac arrest, or suicide.

Both conditions are considered emotional problems. Of the two, bulimia is more common but anorexia is more serious. Often, the two conditions overlap. Half of those with anorexia go on to develop bulimia as well.

Anorexia

A girl with anorexia is a girl who is starving. She is limiting her food intake so severely that she becomes bone-thin. She will not eat, and denies she is hungry—even when she is suffering with terrible hunger pains.

Who Gets Anorexia

The experts don't know why one kid develops anorexia and another doesn't. We are a society that, awash in an abundance of food, holds thinness in the highest regard. This puts a lot of pressure on all young women to be slender.

And so, lots of teenage girls diet. When they successfully reach their target weight, they stop. But sometimes a girl will become obsessive about what she eats, how much she eats, even where she eats. And, no matter how thin she becomes, she still believes she's fat. That girl has developed anorexia.

If her parents, friends, or teachers tell her that she's becoming dangerously thin, she'll scoff. She'll vehemently deny there is any problem with her weight, her diet, or her health—even though it's clear to all that she's a very sick young person.

Doctors say that these girls share certain characteristics. First, they are usually good children. They rarely disobey, they're never any trouble. They also tend to be overachievers, getting good marks in school and excelling in athletics or dance. They are perfectionists.

Signs of Anorexia:

A thin girl, even a very thin girl, is not necessarily a girl with anorexia. How do you know when there's a problem? Consult with your doctor if you note any of these problems:

- A preoccupation with food
- Weighing herself several times a day
- Significant weight loss
- Feeling fat
- Fear of gaining weight
- Dieting despite being thin
- Lack of a monthly period
- Exercising compulsively
- Bingeing and purging

The experts say these kids also seem to have a problem with self-esteem. They live for the love and approval of others because, inside, they don't credit themselves with a lot of value.

In addition, they have a feeling of being powerless. But there is one thing they can control—and that's the amount of food they eat.

Researchers have also learned that many people with bulimia also suffer from depression or Seasonal Affective Disorder.

Scientists also have discovered that anorexia is eight times more common in people having relatives with the disorder, but they have not yet found what the inherited factor might be.

What to Do

Parents must save teenagers with anorexia from themselves. These teens will beg and cry—even lie—to avoid eating and gaining weight.

The most important step toward healing, according to the American Academy of Family Physicians, is for parents to show their daughter how much they love her.

But the very first step should be a call to the family doctor or pediatrician. Your health provider will examine your daughter, then give you the name of a psychiatrist specializing in the problems of adolescence and childhood.

Treatment involves more than just helping your daughter to gain weight. The primary goal is to help her work on the feelings that are causing her eating problems.

Danger Signs of Starvation

Get immediate medical help if you have a daughter with anorexia who develops any of the following:
- Fatigue
- Feeling cold all the time
- Hair loss
- Growth of fine body hair on the face and back
- Dry skin
- Puffy fingers, ankles, and face

Bulimia

A teenager with bulimia is capable of eating huge amounts of food in a very short period of time. She gorges herself, gorges some more, then feels disgusted. She then tries to rid herself of the food by forcing herself to vomit. She also may use laxatives, diuretics, and even enemas to purge her body of the food. In addition, she may try

Signs of Bulimia:

Your daughter may not level with you if she's experiencing bulimic episodes. Here's what to look for if you suspect there may be a problem. Talk to your doctor if you notice any of these signs:

- Frequent fluctuation in weight
- Large amounts of food missing
- Frequent, unusual dental problems
- Using the bathroom frequently after meals
- Evidence of purging, such as calluses on the backs of fingers
- Swollen glands near the jaw
- Abdominal bloating, heartburn
- Depression or mood swings

to work off the food with prolonged, strenuous exercise.

Binge/purge episodes can range from once or twice a week to several times a day.

Unlike a girl with anorexia, one with bulimia knows she has a problem. She knows that her eating habits are unhealthy, but feels unable to control the situation.

Who Gets Bulimia

Research has shown that people with bulimia may have been fat children or have an obese parent. Their parents are also more likely to abuse alcohol than the general population.

Researchers have also learned that many people with bulimia also suffer from depression or Seasonal Affective Disorder—this is a condition in which depression intensifies during the dark winter months.

What to Do

You may have trouble detecting bulimia, because your daughter's weight is probably normal. But if you even suspect bulimia, seek medical help.

The first step is a physical examination to rule out the presence of any diseases that can cause similar symptoms. Talk to your health care provider about finding an eating disorders clinic, where your teen can receive the medications and counseling that will help her return to a normal life.

Bulimia is often treated with antidepressants and cognitive therapy. Cognitive therapy works on the principle that a person can be taught to recognize a pattern of false thinking and change it.

A person with bulimia will learn to recognize any negative thoughts toward eating as those thoughts are occurring. She will then discuss her thoughts with a cognitive therapist. Eventually, she will be able to root out the old, entrenched ideas, and begin a new, healthier pattern of responding to food.

Where to Find Help

Check hospitals or university medical centers for an eating disorders clinic near you, or contact:

National Association of Anorexia Nervosa and Associated Disorders (ANAD)
P.O. Box 7
Highland Park, IL 60035
708/831-3438

Anorexia Nervosa and Related Eating Disorders, Inc. (ANRED)
P.O. Box 5102
Eugene, OR 97405
503/344-1144

American Anorexia/Bulimia Association, Inc. (AABA)
418 E 76th St.
New York, NY 10021
212/734-1114

National Anorexia Aid Society Harding Hospital
1925 E. Dublin Granville Rd.
Columbus, OH 43229
614/436-1112

Bulimia Anorexia Self-Help (BASH)
6125 Clayton Ave. Ste. 215
St. Louis, MO 63139
314/567-4080

Employment

Out of the blue, your teenaged Ben or Jeri announces the desire to get a job. Ben saw a help-wanted sign at the sneaker shop in the mall. He's particularly enticed by the fact that, as an employee, he can get a 10 percent discount on all those fabulously expensive, gotta-have-'em sneaks.

Jeri would like to work as a cashier at 7-11. She wants to start saving for a car.

Embarking on that first job is really passing through an invisible portal that allows an adolescent into the world of working adults. It's a big step for a kid, because that world has attitudes and expectations your teen previously may not have experienced.

"Parents and teachers don't fire teenagers, whereas employers sometimes do," says Mitch Spero, Psy.D., director of Child and Family Psychologists and a licensed psychologist in Plantation, Florida. "Often, good work in the 'real' world isn't given proper acknowledgment. And, the working world isn't always fair."

How can you judge whether your son or daughter will give a job the commitment, even enthusiasm, that the working world expects of employees? How can you decide whether a job is an enhancement or a distraction in your teen's life?

If your teenager is getting good grades, is meeting household curfews, doing

If your teenager gets a job at minimum wage, he or she will soon learn that certain goals can't be reached without first earning a higher education.

chores—in other words, if your teen is basically a decent kid—a job will enhance his or her life, says Dr. Spero.

"For one thing, a job teaches the work ethic," he says. "And these entry-level jobs are certainly a way that teenagers can pay their dues to enter and belong to the working world."

"But it's important for the child to know that working is a privilege. Earning money outside the household is fine, but it must never become a priority above, or go against, the family's values."

Dr. Spero believes that a job can be both a learning experience and a life experience for a teen.

If your teenager gets a job at minimum wage, he or she will soon learn that certain goals can't be reached without first earning a higher education. "That's a learning experience," he says.

But if a teenager wants to explore different areas of employment in order to prepare for the future, that's a life experience, he explains.

"When I was a teenager, I wanted to be a veterinarian. So I took a job in a pet shop, where I earned $2 an hour," Dr. Spero remembers. "I quickly came to the conclusion that I would not have a satisfying future in that level of job, but I might be happy if I earned a doctoral degree, learned business skills, and eventually owned a string of animal hospitals. That was a life experience."

Make a United Front

Before you give the okay for your teenager to seek employment, Dr. Spero recommends that you get together with your spouse to make sure you are of a like mind. Ask yourselves: Do we both approve of a summer job? A part-time job during the school year? Do we both agree that our teenager must maintain a certain grade level? Do we both agree that household chores still must be done regularly?

Want Fries with That?

The following represents the range of jobs your child might find during the summer or after school:

- Sales clerk in the mall
- Fast-food worker
- Amusement park worker
- Summer camp counselor
- Summer resort worker
- Typing or filing in an office

Self-employment opportunities include:

- Babysitting
- Lawn mowing
- Dog walking
- Car washing
- Creating web pages for friends and family
- Tutoring

"It's vital that both parents make this decision," says Dr. Spero. "The danger is when one parent thinks a job is fine, but the other doesn't agree. The child then will side with one parent against the other. It's called triangulation, and it should be avoided."

Once you and your spouse are in agreement, progress to the next step: a written, dated, and signed contract with your teenager.

"The three of you will discuss and agree to how many hours will be worked, what grade average must be maintained, which chores will still be done," he suggests. "Get into the real details, too." For example, if you all agree that a C average must be maintained, will you still allow working if your teenager fails in only a single subject—but manages a C average because of good marks in other subjects?

a teen worker's bill of rights

teenagers have rights under the Fair Labor Standards Act (FLSA) and other laws. The U.S. Department of Labor offers the following guidelines for youngsters who work:

Right One: It Pays to Work—And Work Must Pay

Your teen has the right to a fair and full day's pay for a fair and full day's work, to have hours of work properly recorded, and to be paid at least the federal minimum wage.

Right Two: Overtime Work—Overtime Pay

Your teen has the right to overtime pay (at least time and one half my regular rate of pay) for every hour worked beyond 40 hours a week. (Note: this right arises under the FLSA, which contains significant exemptions for some jobs that teen workers may perform.)

Right Three: Safety Is Part of the Job

Your teen has the right to a safe workplace and the right to file a complaint if the job is unsafe. He or she has the right to required safety clothing, equipment, and training.

Note: Teens under age 18 are prohibited from certain tasks:

- Using power-driven woodworking, hoisting, slicing, or baking machines
- Driving a motor vehicle or being an outside helper on one, except under limited circumstances
- Manufacturing/storing explosives
- Coal mining and other kinds of mining

- Logging/saw-milling
- Being exposed to radioactive substances/ionizing radiation
- Meat packing
- Manufacturing brick, tile, and related products
- Wrecking, demolition, and ship-breaking operations

Limited exceptions apply for some apprentices and student learners. Additional restrictions apply to workers 15 and younger. If under 16, your child's employer is not permitted to have him or her work past 9 p.m. between Labor Day and June 1.

Right Four: No Harassment Hassles

Your teen has the right to equal employment opportunity without regard to race, color, religion, sex, national origin, or disability in an environment free of sexual and physical harassment.

Some states have worker protections which exceed federal standards. Call your state labor department for more information.

Adapted from the U.S. Dept. of Labor's "A Teen Worker's Bill of Rights."

Remain Involved

When your son or daughter actually lands a job, it's important for you and/or your spouse to check it out.

Pay a visit. "Initially, transport your child to and from work, so you can see for yourself what the environment is like," says Dr. Spero. "However, don't embarrass your teenager. Let your teen develop his or her own reputation and individuality."

Know what to look for. You will want to make sure the premises are clean and safe. Look, too, at the other employees. Do they seem like nice people? Are they the kind of folks you want your son or daughter to spend a lot of time with?

Stay attuned. Finally, says Dr. Spero, after your teenager has started working, listen to the way he or she talks about the job. Is it with pleasure and excitement,

"Money should not be the primary goal. The job has to be rewarding in itself, and not just a means to an end. A job should be a way to investigate areas that your child is interested in."

or does the whole experience sound like a dreary ordeal necessary to earn money? Ask your teenager what was the best and the worst part of each working day.

Getting the Most from a Job

"Money," says Dr. Spero, "should not be the primary goal. The job has to be rewarding in itself, and not just a means to an end. A job should be a way to investigate areas that your child is interested in," he says.

Make it a learning experience. Your teenager will be surprised at how much he or she is learning.

Top five things youth ages 13 to 17 report spending their money on.

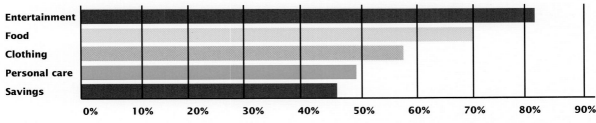

Source: "The Mood of American Youth," The Horatio Alger Association of Distinguished Americans, Inc., Alexandria, VA., 1996.

"A bag boy in a grocery store is learning a lot about social interaction. A kid working in a hardware store will become familiar with using a cash register, making returns, making keys, so many more skills," says Dr. Spero.

"I suggest that a working teen make a resume of all the specific skills learned, in order to secure the next job," he says.

Stick with it. Dr. Spero recommends that your teenager keep a job for "a minimum" of six months.

If your teen leaves before six months, that's a bad reflection on him or her, says Dr. Spero. "The employer has spent time and money in training," he says. (His own resume as a youngster reflected one-year blocks of employment.)

"I learned as much as I could from each mentor, then I moved on," he says.

Always keep in mind that, if a job is having a negative effect on your teen's schoolwork, or if he or she has fallen in with dubious companions, parents have the right to terminate that job, says Dr. Spero.

"Adolescence is the only time period of life when a salaried position will be considered a privilege," he says.

Monitor sleep. You also need to make sure that having a job while still in school is not cutting into your teenager's sleep time. For information on how much sleep a teenager needs, see "Sleep," on page 137.

Fan Clubs and Hero Worship

What teenager hasn't, at least occasionally, engaged in a little hero worship? Whether it was Elvis Presley in the 50s, the Beatles in the 60s, David Cassidy in the 70s, or the Hanson brothers today, a little bit of hero worship seems to come with that territory called adolescence.

Admiration Versus Obsession

There are numerous reasons for hero worship, including a desire to fit in, an outlet for emerging sexual feelings, and help with independence from the family.

And most of the time a little bit of hero worship is both normal and harmless. But there are times when a teen's hero worship may be more worrisome.

teen magazines

adolescents spend a lot of time reading teen magazines. According to one Gallup poll, 62 percent of 13- to 15-year-olds and 52 percent of 16- to 17-year-olds look at magazines daily.

Sometimes parents take the attitude, "Well, at least they're reading!" But what they are reading can be even more important than the fact that they are reading. Research, for example, shows that teens who are frequent readers of fashion magazines are more likely to want to lose weight, are less satisfied with their own bodies, are more frustrated about their weight, and are more fearful of getting fat. Not surprisingly, this can contribute to eating disorders.

And it's not just eating disorders you have to worry about. Believe it or not, some popular teen magazines today include stories about contraceptive use and how to have "great sex." If these are not the values you want your teen to incorporate, you need to set limits on what is acceptable reading material.

The key is to know what your teen is reading. Read some issues yourself, and talk with your teen about the values portrayed in the articles. If you find that your teenager is reading a lot of magazines that espouse values with which you disagree, find alternative magazines that portray more positive values and treat your teen to a subscription.

First, it matters a great deal who the hero is that your adolescent worships. That's because teens tend to want to incorporate the values, attitudes, and behaviors of their hero into their budding search for self. If their heroes project positive values, attitudes, and behaviors, that is what adolescents incorporate.

But if heroes project hate, nihilism, and hopelessness, those are the qualities adolescents will attempt to incorporate. Unfortunately, there are more than a few

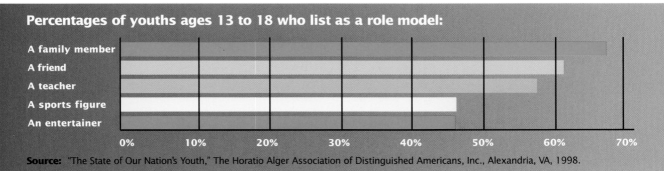

Percentages of youths ages 13 to 18 who list as a role model:

A family member, A friend, A teacher, A sports figure, An entertainer

0% 10% 20% 30% 40% 50% 60% 70%

Source: "The State of Our Nation's Youth," The Horatio Alger Association of Distinguished Americans, Inc., Alexandria, VA, 1998.

instances of teens being "inspired" by their heroes to engage in hateful acts, self-mutilation, and even suicide.

A second problem develops when the hero worship escalates into obsession. Admiring someone is one thing. Becoming obsessed with that person is another thing altogether.

When teens admire someone, they recognize that while there are some things about that person that are admirable, they don't want to be exactly like that person. In other words, admiration implies some psychological distance.

Obsession, in contrast, involves a more complete surrendering of self. Here, teens no longer just admire certain qualities about their heroes, they want to be that person. Usually, this is a signal of very low self-worth. If this happens with your teen, try to divert his or her attention to other activities.

On Being a Fan

A related issue is fan club membership. Although joining a fan club in and of itself is not necessarily an indication of a problem, fan club membership—and especially obsessive fan club membership—is associated with low self-esteem and fear of being viewed in a negative way by others. If this seems to be the case with your teen, try to encourage his or her involvement in other social interests, such as after-school extracurricular activities, sports, and religious youth groups. Make sure spend time praising your teen for all well-done activities.

The bottom line is this: While you shouldn't be too alarmed if your teen engages in a little hero worship or joins a fan club, you should educate yourself as to the messages and values portrayed by the heroes your teen worships and the fan clubs your teen joins. Be prepared to set limits if the messages fall outside of the values you are trying to set or if that admiration turns into full-scale obsession.

Grief

t is as inevitable as sunset at the end of the day. A teenager will at some point lose grandparents, a beloved pet, or a good friend, and sometimes even suffer the tragedy of losing a parent. The immutable fact is that every one of us will grieve for a loved one.

Adults have lived long enough to know the leaden weight of grief. It is never welcome. Grownups have generally learned to cope. But how do parents help their teens (and their children) get through their first encounter with the death of a person they love?

"The number one thing: Don't make death from Day One a forbidden topic," says Henry J. Gault, M.D., a spokesperson for the American Academy of Child and Adolescent Psychology and a professor of child and adolescent psychology at the University of Illinois in Grayslake.

Dealing with Death and Dying

"Death is part of life," says Dr. Gault. "We may not always be comfortable with that thought—or even like it—but in that perspective death is natural. By seeing death as a part of life, it's easier to talk about."

In fact, Dr. Gault recommends that parents look for opportunities to discuss death. If a famous entertainer, a sports figure, or a politician dies, you can talk to your teenager about the death of that person in the context of the life they lived. Talk

"Death is part of life. We may not always be comfortable with that thought—or even like it—but in that perspective death is natural. By seeing death as a part of life, it's easier to talk about."

about that person's good deeds, achievements, and the ways that person made things better for the people around them. Suggest that a life well lived, the life of a good person, is an accomplishment.

"If your children express concern about death, if they seem to be worried, tell them that, indeed, everyone does die—but that it happens when we are much older," says Dr. Gault.

And so, if a family member is very ill, it's important to be open about sharing that information with your teenager. Whether Grandma and Grandpa live across town or halfway across the country, they are special people to your teen and their passing will be painful.

You might say something like, "Gramma is pretty sick, and she doesn't seem to be getting better. The doctor says that she may die. We hope not, but we shouldn't be surprised if that happens."

This sort of conversation provides your teenager with a chance to ask questions and talk about death before it actually happens.

Attending a Funeral

Should Grandma die, advises Dr. Gault, encourage your teen to attend the wake and the funeral, and to go to the cemetery. Parents whose kids are left at home may think they are protecting them, but this is not protecting them at all. "Probably they are protecting themselves—from being overwhelmed by their children's terrible sadness," says Dr. Gault.

A 10-year-old can have upsetting fantasies about the rituals of dying, wondering what could be so terrible that he or she isn't allowed to be part of it. But if your adolescent attends the funeral, then the young person becomes very much a part of your family's involvement. It also helps the adolescent experience the solemnity of closure. Just as for adults, attending funerals helps youngsters put the experience of death behind them and move forward.

As long as Mom and Dad are around to maintain an adolescent's security, the young family member can handle the experience, says Dr. Gault.

"But use your judgment," he says. If your teenager refuses to attend, do not force the issue. But do encourage your teenager to spend some time with the rest of the family as they say goodbye.

Death of a Parent

If you are a surviving parent, you can see clearly that your teenager's world has been shattered.

Be soft; be firm. In the midst of your own grieving, it can be difficult—but it is imperative—for you to open your heart to your son or daughter. Your teen's loss is at least as great as your own. Because your teenager's sense of security is toppling, you must make yourself a rock to lean on.

Lend an ear. More than that, you must be ready to help your teen heal by listening. Let your son or daughter talk about feelings—about losing Mom or Dad, about fears and concerns.

When a parent dies, the child feels enormous sadness, of course. But he or she also may feel anger or fear and, often, depression, says Dr. Gault.

Allow for different responses. Each teenager is different, of course, and may react in different ways. "Some react with denial and seem not to be responding to the death at all. But of course, they are," says Dr. Gault. "Some react with anxiety. They have problems sleeping. They have a loss of appetite." Other children are irritable, or they isolate themselves from their friends. They may be less motivated at school and have trouble concentrating.

Saying Goodbye to Bowser

He was always there, faithful dog, tail thumping on the floor with joy at the sight of the school bus coming home. He was always there, with a comforting lick, with a dog-breath nuzzle for the child who felt lonely or blue. He was always there, to run like the wind after a tennis ball, to clown and pant through any game.

And then, one day, he wasn't there.

With tears streaming from your own eyes and pain grabbing at your throat, how will you face your teenagers? What can you say to help them through the loss of their dear old pal?

"The way you handle the death of a pet can be a model for what's to come in life," says Henry J. Gault, M.D. "Come together as a family to support each other and to mark the pet's passing. Bury the pet, or have a memorial service for him."

"Encourage your kids to 're-enjoy' the good times they had with their dog," he says.

So take out the snapshots of Bowser when he was a puppy, show the video of him playing Frisbee with Dad, reminisce about the time he chased the "cat" that was really a skunk.

Keeping a pet alive in that way makes it easier for your teens to deal with his death, according to Dr. Gault.

Stay with the process. To help a teenager through this tragedy, Dr. Gault suggests that the surviving parent remain available. As the days and weeks pass, help your teen express anger or fear. Counter some of the sadness by recalling good times the family had in the past.

Get help if you need to. If the surviving parent is so overcome with grief that he or she can't cope with the emotional needs of a teenager, then that teen will be washed alone into a sea of uncertainty and unhappiness.

In such a case, other adults should step in to be there for the teen. "An aunt, an uncle, a grandparent, even a neighbor, can make things much better," says Dr. Gault.

Waiting for Sunrise

In the days after the funeral, life resumes some of its old rhythm—back to work, back to school, dinner, dishes, homework, bedtime. On the surface everything seems the same, but in reality everything is totally different. Hearts are heavy. Food tastes like ashes. The simplest task is a chore. When will it end?

It takes six months to a year for teenagers—for any children—to come to terms with the death of someone they loved. "That's the acute phase of grieving," says Dr. Gault. "It takes that long for symptoms such as sleeplessness or loss of appetite to return to normal."

It is extremely important, the doctor says, that you encourage communication during this time. Get your kids to talk about what they feel. "Eventually, they will have a healthy acceptance," says Dr. Gault. "They will reintegrate, and with renewed energy be able to move on."

"But if, after a year, your child still seems isolated, is still not sleeping well, then it's time to seek professional help," he says.

Headaches

I f your son or daughter comes dragging home from school complaining of a headache, don't be alarmed. As long as your teenager is healthy, there is no immediate reason to worry. Headaches are fairly common among older children and teens, say the doctors at the Mayo Clinic.

The Tension Headache

A typical, run-of-the-mill headache is called a tension headache or a muscle contraction headache. It feels like a tight band around the head, or a weight pressing down on it. The pain is usually centered in the scalp, temples, or back of the neck. It is dull and steady, but not throbbing.

The causes of a tension headache are numerous. Maybe your son is hungry. Maybe your daughter needs glasses. Maybe she's tired. These all are possible causes of tension headaches, but the most likely cause is stress and/or anxiety.

The usual treatment, of course, is a painkiller such as aspirin, acetaminophen, or ibuprofen. Give your teenager medication according to the package instructions, then settle him or her in a comfortable, quiet place. In less than an hour, the pain should begin to ebb away.

If you prefer to avoid medications whenever possible, there are a few remedies you can try first. Tell your teenager to take a nice hot shower, aiming the spray at the back of the neck and shoulders. (This treatment is particularly effective with a showerhead massager.) Cold also does the trick. Place a cold, wet cloth, an ice bag, or even a bag of frozen peas on the nape of the neck for natural relief. Taking a nap also helps.

Tension headaches are no big deal, unless your teenager complains of headaches frequently. If that is the case, you'll need to do two things. First, have a doctor check out the situation to rule out any physical problems that may be causing the

The causes of a tension headache are numerous. Maybe your son is hungry. Maybe your daughter needs glasses. Maybe she's tired.

headaches. When you get the all-clear from your physician, then start working on the cause of these tension headaches.

What is troubling your daughter or son? Is his day overscheduled? Is he fatigued? Is there a problem with her grades? With friends? With that special friend?

Armed with exquisite tact, broach the subject of what's bothering your teenager. Listen, and don't interrupt. The problem may be a simple one that resolves itself (the pressure of final exams) or a more complex one (the pressure to go steady). Whatever it may be, take the opportunity to help your teen put the problem in perspective. Perhaps, together, you can work out a solution.

Migraine Headaches

Migraines begin to kick in during late childhood and the teen years, particularly at puberty. In fact, the peak onset is between 8 and 12 years of age for boys, and between 13 and 17 years for girls.

Although migraines can strike both sexes, three out of four people who experience them are female. Migraines also seem to run in families. In fact, most people who get migraines know at least one other family member with the same problem.

You can suspect a migraine headache if your teenager experiences a morning headache with a throbbing pain in one side of the head. Your teen may complain of nausea and of sensitivity to light or loud noises. Typically, the pain starts in or around the eye, or the temple. It often becomes more severe with physical activity—even just bending over.

Some migraines are preceded by a virtual light show, called an

When to Call the Doctor

Most headaches are no big deal. There are circumstances, however, in which headaches need medical attention. Call the doctor if you see any of these signs with your teenager's headache:

- Follows a blow to the head

- Lasts longer than 24 hours and does not respond to a pain reliever

- Is so severe it interrupts daily activities

- Is accompanied by dizziness, clumsiness, or vision problems

- Recurs with increasing frequency

- Feels different from previous headaches

- Is accompanied by a stiff neck and fever (a sign of meningitis)

aura. About 20 minutes before the throbbing begins, your teenager may complain of seeing sparkling flashes of light, of rainbow colors, and of a blind spot that grows larger in the field of vision.

Doctors think a migraine happens when arteries to the brain constrict, then dilate. They don't know why the arteries squeeze then open, but they suspect the trigger may be abnormally low blood levels of a chemical called serotonin.

Watch for food clues. These headaches may be brought on by dietary habits. Missing a meal can lead to one. Eating foods with MSG, aged cheeses, chocolate, citrus fruits, and preserved meats also may be a trigger. Start paying attention to what your teenager was eating before the migraine began. With these dietary culprits in mind, you may be able to prevent future problems.

Mind those moods. They also can be brought on by stress, anxiety, and especially by depression. Stay alert for clues to the mood/migraine connection. If your teenager knows that stress, for example, triggers a migraine, then finding ways to relax in stressful times will become a priority.

Migranes can be brought on by stress, anxiety, and especially by depression. Stay alert for clues to the mood/migraine connection.

Stick to a sleep schedule. Your teen can help lessen the frequency of these headaches by keeping a consistent sleep pattern, getting up and going to bed at the same time every day—even on Saturday and Sunday. Those that love the feel of sleeping in may have to settle instead for a cat nap later in the day.

Steer clear of indoor pollution. It really does help to avoid cigarette smoke.

Keep a record. It may also help for your teen to keep a headache diary. He or she should keep track of when the migraines occur and note what was eaten the previous day, any changes in sleep schedule, whether fatigued or not, or if there was unusual stress.

By noting these details, your son or daughter may be able to pinpoint exactly what triggers those migraines.

Try medication. These headaches can be treated with a variety of prescription medications. The old standby is ergotamine, which aborts a migraine. Newer drugs include Migranal NS, which delivers pain relief as a nasal spray.

Some new medicines soon will be available to prevent migraines, including calcium channel blockers and a form of Prozac, according to the National Headache Foundation.

One over-the-counter medication—Excedrin Migraine—became available in 1998 for the treatment of mild to moderate migraines.

Stay informed. For more information about both tension and migraine headaches call the National Headache Foundation, 800/843-2256; or the American Council for Headache Education, 800/255-ACHE (800/255-2243).

Low Self-Esteem

Self-esteem is the term used to describe the way people value themselves. Teens with low self-esteem don't think they're worth much and often are too quick to accept and internalize the put-downs of their family and peers. In their own minds, teens with low self-esteem are saying, "I'm worthless," or, "The people around me see me as worthless."

People with low self-esteem have "extreme difficulty" in feeling secure and significant, says Mitch Spero, Psy. D., director of Child and Family Psychologists, a group that specializes in the problems of children and adolescents. A psychologist in Plantation, Florida, Dr. Spero has facilitated a biweekly support group for people with self-esteem problems.

People with low self-esteem "have a sense that they can't keep up; they're just not good enough," he says. "They simply 'can't cut it.'"

The problem with low self-esteem often begins in early childhood. Dr. Spero says these kids may feel rejected by a parent or other caregiver.

"There are many, many different parenting styles," he says. "But two particular ways of parenting seem to lead to low self-esteem in children. One way is to be overly harsh and critical. The child learns to believe that nothing he does is good enough, and begins to think, 'So why even try?'"

"The other parenting style that leads to self-esteem problems is one that

too much of a good thing

believe it or not, it is possible to have too much self-esteem. Contrary to the popular belief that violent behavior is the result of too low self-esteem, violent behavior is actually more likely to result from too high an opinion of oneself.

It seems that individuals with an inflated sense of themselves tend to perceive any criticism or failure experience as an unacceptable attack on their high self-opinion. Their response: lash out at the critic. In fact, studies show that adolescent boys who score extremely high on tests of self-esteem are the very ones who get into the most trouble.

There are even some experts—such as University of Pennsylvania professor and past president of the American Psychological Association Martin Seligman, Ph.D.—who believe that too much emphasis on building self-esteem is a cause for the increasing number of teens experiencing serious depression. Having been told as children that everything they did was "terrific," these teens are prone to depression, when they suddenly discover that not everything they do is, in fact, terrific.

Too high self-esteem results when parents and teachers confuse self-esteem and competence. It's one thing to praise effort and success. But effusive praise unconnected in any meaningful way to actual performance only makes kids think they are more skilled than they really are.

The best defense against creating an overly inflated self-opinion in your teenager, while still helping your teen build healthy self-esteem, is to help your son or daughter build real skills. The idea is that teenagers must experience competence and not just hear that they are competent.

over-builds a child's confidence," says Dr. Spero. That child soon turns into an adolescent who comes to view himself or herself as invincible, and that's bound to lead to problems, he says.

Dr. Spero warns that issues of self-esteem intensify in preadolescence: "In the fourth to sixth grades children are constantly competing with each other. In fact, preadolescence is one of the most competitive periods in our lives. Boys constantly compare who is taller, who is better at sports, who gets the best grades. Girls are constantly judging themselves against others, usually about which girl has the most friends. A child can feel squelched by this kind of environment."

Your Teen's Sense of Worth

If you suspect your teenager may have some self-esteem issues, Dr. Spero suggests you might ask yourself these questions:

- Does your teen choose to be around others in social situations, or does he or she seek isolation?
- Does your teen avoid team activities or other competitive situations?
- Does your teen have a negative attitude about school?
- Does your teen have initiative, coming up with things to do? Or do you hear excuses as to why initiatives won't work?

"Parents should keep their eyes on the kids who play what I call the 'Yes, but ...' game, thwarting any suggestion a parent might make," says Dr. Spero.

The games goes like this:

"Would you like to go bowling?" a parent might ask.

The teen might answer, "Yes, but ... the leagues have all the lanes reserved."

"Wouldn't you like to go to the movies with Valerie?"

"Yes, but ... her mother can't pick us up in time."

Teens with low self-esteem also have difficulty trusting the word of another, says Dr. Spero. "If someone says, 'I'll call you on Friday night,' their reaction is a sarcastic, 'Yeah, sure you will,'" he explains. "They simply don't believe others could value spending time with them."

Some kids with self-esteem problems have difficulty sleeping and experience changes in appetite or energy level. Often these teenagers avoid making decisions.

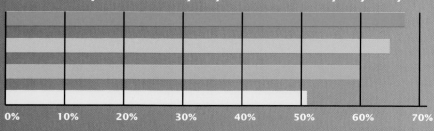

Percentage of 12- to 17-year-olds who report that 'every day' or 'almost every day' they:

Get a hug or a kiss from a parent
Get a compliment or encouraging word from adults
Come across teachers who really care about their students
Get help or advice from parents about homework or school

0%   10%   20%   30%   40%   50%   60%   70%

Source: "Kids These Days: What Americans Really Think About the Next Generation," Public Agenda, New York, NY., 1997.

They reason that if they don't make a decision they can't make a mistake.

"Oddly, they also fear success because they feel they don't deserve all the good things that come with success," he says.

"People with low self-esteem are more likely to blame others, or even circumstances, when something goes wrong," says Dr. Spero. "They must learn to take full responsibility for their actions. In fact, they must learn to turn their mistakes into lessons—to learn something from making that mistake, and then move on."

Parents Can Help

You as a parent can provide a great deal of help and support to a teenager with self-esteem problems.

Encourage activities. It's a good idea for your teenager to become involved in noncompetitive activities, where he or she can interact cooperatively with others. Consider Girl Scouts, Boy Scouts, religious activities, the school orchestra, or glee club. Then tell your teen, "Do your best, but recognize that others may be better."

Often these teenagers with low self-esteem avoid making decisions. They reason that if they don't make a decision they can't make a mistake.

"I read once," says Dr. Spero, "that the gymnast Cathy Rigby's mother told her, 'It's not important to be the best. It's important to do your best.' That's the attitude you want to reinforce."

Communicate. If you suspect that your teen's self-esteem is subterranean, take a risk and ask about it. A good starting question is: "How do you really feel about yourself?" "Listen to the answer with an open mind—without negative perceptions," says Dr. Spero.

It can be helpful to a teenager just to know that someone cares and understands.

Get help, if you need to. If the problem is serious—or even if you're not really sure—consider seeing a psychologist. Many parents hesitate because they think they will be blamed or made to feel guilty. "That's not the case," says Dr. Spero. "Asking for help is more a sign of strength than of weakness."

Mononucleosis

the medical name for this disease is infectious mononucleosis, but it's usually called simply "mono." It's also known as "the kissing disease," and with good reason.

The vast majority of cases—90 percent—are simple and uncomplicated viral infections, says the National Institutes of Health (NIH). Even though mono can be debilitating, it's not considered a serious disease except in rare cases.

Most cases of mono are caused by the Epstein-Barr virus (EBV), a member of the herpes virus family. The rest are caused by the Cytomegalovirus (CMV).

But mono is—both literally and figuratively—a pain in the neck. It lasts a long time, and teenagers become sick and tired of feeling sick and tired. If you have a teen in your family dealing with mono, you will have to try hard to be supportive and understanding during this period.

The prime time for mono is the teen years, especially between 15 and 17. The NIH says that both boys and girls get it, but that boys are infected slightly more often.

Once someone has an EBV infection, the virus remains in the body for life. Fortunately, a healthy immune system usually keeps it under control.

Doctors say that the infection is probably transmitted by saliva. The virus infects and reproduces in the salivary glands. It also infects a type of white blood cells known as B cells. Direct contact with virus-infected saliva, such as through kissing or sharing drinks, can transmit the virus and result in mono. In rare instances, the virus has been transmitted by blood transfusion.

How Do You Know It's Mono?

Mono is a slow disease—slow to develop and slow to clear up. Symptoms may take between two and seven weeks to develop after exposure to the virus. The virus hangs around for a long time. It can be found in the saliva of most people who have had mono for at least six months after the acute infection has subsided.

If your teenager has mono, you'll at first hear complaints of vague symptoms like fatigue, chilliness, malaise, muscle aches, and/or a loss of appetite.

Later, the more obvious symptoms appear:
- Sore throat
- Swollen lymph glands, especially at the side and back of the neck, but also under the arm and in the groin
  - Enlarged tonsils covered with a yellowish- white material
- A pink rash that looks something like measles (One in five kids with mono experiences this particular symptom.)

Your teenager will develop a fever of 101 to 105 degrees. It usually lasts for five to ten days, but sometimes continues intermittently for as long as three weeks. (A high fever late in the illness suggests bacterial complications.)

About half of those with mono have an enlarged spleen, and 20 percent also have an enlarged liver.

The swollen lymph glands and spleen heal in about a month. Fatigue may linger for two to three months.

Less frequently occurring symptoms include:

- Rapid heart rate
- Sensitivity to light
- Shortness of breath
- Irregular heart rate
- Headache
- Hives
- Cough
- Jaundice
- Neck stiffness
- Nosebleed
- Chest pain

Seeing the Doctor

The doctor will tell you that your teenager doesn't have to be isolated. In fact, your teen probably was infectious for several days before symptoms appeared.

First on the agenda is a physical exam, where the doctor checks for an enlarged spleen and/or liver. These organs may feel tender when the doctor gently presses. The doctor also will check for swollen glands and a skin rash.

But the real giveaway that your teen has mono is a blood test. One part of the test counts a type of white blood cells known as lymphocytes, to see if they have increased in number. The test also spots unusual looking lymphocytes, cells that are activated and fighting the infection. These may show in the blood for two to eight weeks. The test also checks for the antibodies that form against EBV. At the same time the doctor also checks the blood for abnormalities of liver function, which are also characteristic of the disease.

If the test is negative, but your is teen still ill, the doctor probably will do additional tests to rule out other infections.

Diagnosing mono is about all modern medicine can do for this disease. There is no medication to treat it. Your teen will recover within four to six weeks.

What doctors do prescribe is rest, and analgesics such as acetaminophen or ibuprofen to relieve pain and fever. Skip the aspirin, please, because it can increase the risk of Reye's syndrome, a potentially fatal condition that can develop in both children and teenagers from taking aspirin while having a fever.

Salt water gargles can help the sore throat. (Use ½ teaspoon of salt in a glass of warm water several times a day.)

Years ago, the standard treatment was bed rest for four to six weeks, with limited activity for three months after all symptoms had passed. Today, doctors usually only recommend avoiding strenuous exercise. That's because a real hazard is the possibility of damaging the enlarged spleen. Your teenager must avoid lifting, straining, and competitive sports until the recovery is complete. Your doctor also may suggest a high protein, decreased fat diet and vitamin supplements.

Get Help Immediately If...

Go to the emergency room or call 911 if your teenager has mono and experiences a sharp, sudden pain in the left upper abdomen. This pain may indicate a rapidly enlarging or even a rupturing spleen.

The occurrence is rare, but when it happens, it requires emergency surgery.

Overweight

We are a nation of fatties. And we are raising the next generation of fatties. Hard words? Perhaps. But that's the word from the national Centers for Disease Control and Prevention.

An analysis from the most recent National Health and Nutrition Examination Survey, conducted in the early 90s, found that approximately 14 percent of children ages 6 to 11 are overweight, and that 12 percent of adolescents ages 12 to 17 are also too heavy.

Those figures are bad enough, but when compared to the previous government surveys done in the 60s and 70s, they are shocking. In those days, only 5 percent of our children were overweight.

What happened?

Doctors at the Mayo Clinic and other experts studying the problem of obesity

getting medical help

Your family doctor or pediatrician—who has kept your teen's height and weight charts since childhood and knows your teen's medical history—can estimate the weight your son or daughter should be.

The first step usually is to determine just how much of your teen's body is composed of fat.

Weighing on a scale doesn't tell the whole story because muscle is heavier than fat. A prizefighter with bulging muscles can tip the scales as a heavyweight, but he is not fat.

The official, scientific way to measure a person's body fat is to do it underwater. That, however, requires a laboratory with special equipment.

Your family doctor, instead, may measure skinfold thickness and do a bioelectrical impedance analysis (BIA).

To measure skinfold thickness the doctor will use a special instrument—much like calipers—to grab a pinch of skin at certain targeted parts of the body. These are parts where fat tends to accumulate, such as the back of the upper arm, the abdomen, thigh, and so forth. The amount of flesh that's held in the instrument (an inch, 2 inches) allows the doctor to estimate the percentage of fat in the body.

The next step may be the BIA, which sends a harmless amount of electrical current through the body. The current reveals the amount of water in the body. Generally, a higher percentage of water indicates a larger amount of muscle and lean tissue.

The doctor then will do the math, translating the percent of water into an estimate of body fat and lean body mass.

Your doctor also may employ "body mass index measures." The body mass index is found by dividing a person's weight in kilograms by height in meters squared.

After all is pinched and prodded, your doctor may say something like this to your teenager: "Mary (or Joe), I've estimated how much of your body is made up of fat, and it would be good for you to replace some of that fat with lean muscle. By exercising and watching what you eat, you should comfortably be able to lose about a pound a week. At the same time, your body is growing—so you should start looking and feeling much better in just a few months."

Your doctor will not recommend diet pills or a starvation diet. Instead the recommendation will be to avoid fatty foods and to do 30 minutes of moderate physical activity every day.

all point to lifestyle as the primary cause of excessive weight gain.

If you are the parent of a teenager who is a little too well rounded, you may be puzzled by the cause of his or her excess weight. You serve normal meals, and there is no evidence that your teen is wolfing down fattening foods.

Indeed, your teen may be eating "normal" amounts of food, but nevertheless consuming too many calories for his or her sedentary ways to burn up.

It's a simple formula: If you consume more calories than you burn, you inevitably will gain weight.

Get 'Em Moving

Is your teenager too sedentary? There's a pretty good chance that this is the case. Nationwide, our kids tend to be more inactive than in previous years. They spend more time in front of the television, and—lately—more hours playing computer games or surfing the Net.

In her report on physical activity and health, the Surgeon General Donna Shalala, M.D., says that nearly half of young people aged 12 to 21 are not vigorously active on a regular basis.

Dr. Shalala also says that physical activity "declines dramatically with age during adolescence," and that girl teens are much less physically active than boy teens.

Sure, say the experts, there can be a genetic predisposition to becoming overweight, but that predisposition has not changed in the last 30 years. Yet the percentage of overweight kids has ballooned.

Tackle the Problem

Some parents shrug off the problem of weight, thinking that, as their kids grow, the situation will resolve itself. But that's rarely true.

Eighty percent of children who are obese between the ages of 10 and 13 will be obese when they are adults, say doctors at the Mayo Clinic. And that means health problems down the road— problems like diabetes, high blood pressure, gallbladder disease, breathing problems, some forms of cancer, and more.

Ten Low-Cal Snacks Your Kids Will Love

1 A skim milk and banana smoothie
2 A frosty dish of diced melon
3 A rice cake smeared with reduced-fat peanut butter
4 Frozen seedless grapes
5 Any flavor of fat-free yogurt
6 A celery stalk stuffed with low-fat cream cheese
7 A handful of carrot "coins"
8 Fruit cocktail of diced apple and sliced banana dressed with orange juice
9 A cup of diet gelatin
10 A small green salad with no-fat dressing or lemon juice

Then there's the social stigma. Heavy teens usually are not very good at sports, and so they don't get picked for any teams. Heavy teens are often not considered cute by the opposite sex and don't get invited to parties or out on dates. Heavy teens are discriminated against when applying for jobs and even for college admissions.

Add to that the knowledge that there's hardly anyone more miserable, more filled with self-loathing, than a fat teenager, and you'll clearly see the need to step in and help your child.

Step-by-Step Action

Some weight-loss counselors suggest that you, Mom and Dad, take the very first step.

Gather information. For one week, keep a diary of your teen's physical activities and everything that he or she eats. Ask questions, and be frank about your reasons for being so inquisitive. You may learn that the school's physical education classes are few and short in duration. Or that the time spent at basketball practice was actually time spent sitting on the bench.

Also the munchies may strike on the way home from school—which is also on the way past the pizza shop or ice cream stand. Or just before bed, when tired kids grab any snack that's convenient. (Read cookies or chips.)

Plan some changes. Once armed with this information, you can begin to make moderate changes in your teen's eating and activity patterns. If possible, make this a family project. Your teenager will have an easier time of it if he or she doesn't have to watch others at the table eat with abandon.

You might, for example, serve only enough food for only one helping; toss any fatty snacks, such as chips, in the trash, and replace them with fruits and vegetables; or cut out desserts for everyone. For complete information on providing nutritional meals and snacks to your hungry teenager, see Chapter 2, "Feed Me," which begins on page 23.

Work toward the right attitude. Make clear to your teenager that this change in lifestyle is not a form of punishment. It is not a painful repentance for being bad, for overeating, and for getting fat.

Instead, encourage your teen to think of these changes in eating and exercise patterns as useful tools—tools that will help him or her achieve a desired goal.

Keep your teenager on track with a weekly weigh-in. Remember, the goal is to lose only a pound or so each week. Join your teenager in applauding the disappearance of every ounce of fat. Rejoice over the firmer arms or tighter tummy.

Introduce exercise. Next, introduce a little physical activity— like shooting hoops after dinner, or taking Rover for a good, long walk. Select an activity that your teenager will enjoy, and one that fits in with daily life.

Encourage your teen to exercise for about a half hour every day. Such regular physical activity not only helps to control weight, but also helps build healthy bones, muscles, and joints, and also promotes a sense of well-being.

Don't be a drill sergeant. Avoid launching into a full-blown Paris Island Boot Camp routine. It'll exhaust your kid and ultimately backfire. Besides, it's simply not necessary.

Even the simplest exercise does the trick. Your teen will burn nearly the same number of calories, for example, walking a mile

Getting Physical

The less vigorous an exercise is, the longer it has to be done to gain any real benefit. The list below suggests several moderate exercises, in order of intensity, along with recommended times.

- Playing volleyball for 45 minutes

- Playing touch football for 30 to 45 minutes

- Walking 1¾ miles in 35 minutes

- Shooting baskets for 30 minutes

- Bicycling 5 miles in 30 minutes

- Fast social dancing for 30 minutes

- Swimming laps for 20 minutes

- Playing basketball for 15 to 20 minutes

as he or she would running a mile. Walking just takes twice as long.

Provide plenty of opportunities for physical activity. A summer picnic that includes a nice bike ride through the park or a swim in the lake is ideal. A family rake-a-thon of fallen leaves is good, too. Keep the back of your mind humming on ways to build exercise into your teen's day.

Premenstrual Syndrome (PMS)

"honey, I don't think you should wear that skirt to school. It's a little too short," Mother might venture. "Why are you always picking on me?" Julia counters. "You never let me wear what I want to," she sobs. "You want me to look like a geek!"

With tears streaming down her red and scrunched-up face, Julia storms back to her room. "You're awful! I hate you," she yells, punctuating the statement by pounding her feet on the stairs.

Mother sighs. She knows that Julia loves her very much. But in the last few months she has seen occasions when her daughter has become angry and out of control for no good reason. Julia is moody and obviously irritated by something. Could her problem be PMS?

Yes it could, say the doctors at the PMS Program at the University of Pennsylvania Medical Center in Philadelphia.

While premenstrual syndrome is most common among women who are in their twenties and thirties, it can occur just about any time between the onset of menstruation and menopause.

PMS is a complex problem, and the symptoms women with PMS experience are real—not just "all in the head."

Fifty years ago, medical books did not even mention the topic. But times have changed, and now doctors know that PMS is an actual condition that most likely is caused by monthly fluctuations in the body's levels of the hormones estrogen and progesterone.

Pinpointing the Problem

How can you and your daughter discover whether she actually has PMS?

There are no laboratory tests for the syndrome, so there is no black-and-white determination of whether the problem exists. Instead, a doctor must rely on your daughter's description of how she feels in order to make the diagnosis.

The number one marker for PMS is that the problem is cyclical. That is, whatever symptoms your daughter suffers show up at about the same time every month, then go away.

There are four common patterns. In the first, symptoms appear five to seven days before the onset of the period and subside with menstruation. In the second, symptoms begin at ovulation (usually the fourteenth day of the cycle) and last about two weeks, or until menstruation begins. In the third pattern, symptoms begin at ovulation and last up to three weeks, until the period is nearly over. Fourth, symptoms appear for a few days at ovulation then go away, only to return several days before the period begins.

Your doctor most likely will ask your daughter to keep a daily calendar to record her symptoms. She will be asked to keep track of her symptoms for a good two or three months.

Not only does the calendar help the doctor to make a diagnosis, it also can help your daughter to clearly see that her problems come (and go!) in a predictable way. Often, that knowledge alone is enough to reassure your daughter that she's not losing her mind.

Taking Control

Most cases of PMS can be controlled with diet, exercise, and stress-control techniques. But it's always best to begin with a doctor visit, if for no other reason than to rule out any other possible causes of the symptoms.

Of course, you should follow the doctor's recommendations to the letter.

Focus on diet. A good first step (after the visit to the doctor) is to improve your daughter's diet. Start by eliminating salt and sugar from family meals and urging her to follow through with meals eaten away from home. Salt causes the body to retain water and can result in bloating. Refined sugar wreaks havoc with blood sugar levels, resulting in energy levels that bounce up and down like a yo-yo.

In your menu planning, emphasize complex carbohydrates, such as fresh fruit, vegetables, and whole grains.

Consider caffeine. Many doctors also recommend eliminating caffeine from the diet. That means eliminating not only coffee, but also colas, tea, iced tea, and even chocolate.

Eat less, more often. Also suggest that your daughter eat a little less at breakfast, lunch, and dinner, so that she can have after-school and bedtime snacks. These smaller, more frequent meals will help fight lethargy and fatigue by keeping blood sugar levels on an even keel.

Look into vitamins. Ask your doctor, too, about the advisability of giving your daughter vitamin B supplements,

The Bloat, the Blues, the Blahs

PMS symptoms vary among teenage girls. Some girls experience mild distress, while others are nearly incapacitated.

The symptoms themselves are all over the place. In fact, more than 100 have been noted. The most common include:

- Depression
- Fatigue
- Feelings of being out of control
- Irritability
- Lethargy
- Unexplained anger

In addition, girls may experience:

- Acne
- Bloating
- Back pain
- Clumsiness
- Compulsive eating
- Craving sweet or salty food
- Eye problems
- Headaches
- Joint pain
- Weight gain

Other symptoms include:

- Bowel problems, such as constipation or diarrhea
- Crying
- Paranoia
- Poor concentration
- Seizures
- Suicidal thoughts
- Violence

Please note: Some of the symptoms listed here are serious. Do not assume that something like a seizure, an episode of violence, or suicidal thoughts can be dismissed as "mere PMS." Always discuss such symptoms with a doctor.

particularly vitamin B6. The doctor will recommend the proper dosage, if supplementation seems in order.

Get moving. Exercise, doctors say, is a natural mood elevator and an excellent stress reliever. They suggest exercising for about one-half hour at least three times a week. An aerobic workout would be excellent. Bicycling is a good choice, as is swimming. But remember, a brisk walk works well.

Deal with stress. Stressful situations seem ever so much worse to someone with PMS. Of course, no one can eliminate stress from life, but almost everyone can learn better ways to cope with it.

When your daughter feels like the world is closing in on her, suggest that she try deep breathing, meditation, or prayer. It also works to visualize a peaceful environment. All these techniques can take the sting out of stress.

And don't forget the mother of all stress-relief techniques—the nap. A little snooze is especially helpful if your daughter has had trouble sleeping.

Seek medical treatment. If your daughter's case is severe, a doctor may suggest medications. Diuretics, by helping the body eliminate excess water, can help lessen bloating and swelling. Oral contraceptives, prescribed as a means of regulating hormones, often help relieve a wide variety of symptoms. The doctor may recommend a mild tranquilizer to take the edge off feelings of anger and tension.

The Ins and Outs of a PMS Diet

The Premenstrual Institute recommends that certain foods be eliminated in a PMS diet, while other foods are emphasized. Here are the ins and outs of a successful diet.

In

Fresh fruit, fish, poultry, leafy green vegetables, cereals, fruit juice, mineral water

Out

Candy, chocolate, pastry, ice cream, red meat, sausage, sardines, cold cuts, pastrami, sauerkraut, pickles, olives, relish, potato chips, taco chips, pretzels, cola, coffee, tea

Sibling Rivalry

almost 80 percent of us grow up with at least one brother or sister. That makes sibling relationships among the most important any of us will ever have.

When things go well, siblings provide us with support, encouragement, friendship, and camaraderie. And not just when we are children, but also when we are adults. Indeed, adult happiness is largely dependent upon a supportive network of extended family, the seeds for which are sown in the day-to-day interactions of siblings during childhood.

Unfortunately, sibling relationships are also among the most competitive we will ever experience. Ever since Cain and Abel, siblings have been competing with each other for status, for power, and for affection. As such, sibling rivalry can be an enormous source of frustration for parents.

Being exposed to arguing, complaining, whining, and tattling is never pleasant. It is even less so when it occurs within the context of the family, a place where we are suppose to encounter respite, not bitterness.

Keeping the Peace

Fortunately, there are ways to effectively manage sibling rivalry. Here's what you can do:

Don't compare. A primary reason for sibling rivalry is plain old-fashioned jealousy. Comparing one sibling with another in their presence only builds resentment and encourages further competition. If you must make comparisons, do so in private, and even then only with your spouse.

Set some fighting rules. Be clear on what are acceptable, and what are unacceptable, ways of expressing disagreements. Expecting siblings never to have disagreements is like expecting the sun will someday rise in the west. In other words, it ain't gonna happen.

The key to managing sibling rivalry is not to demand its absence, but to set its ground rules. Be clear on what you will allow, such as expressing verbally (and in a moderate tone) dissatisfaction or frustration with the behavior of a sibling. Also make clear what you will not allow—such things as hitting or name-calling.

Don't be too quick to step in. When your kids argue or experience conflict, give them some time to figure out how best to resolve the conflict on their own. This way, sibling conflict becomes a potential learning experience in how to manage and resolve disagreements. If you jump in too quickly, they will come to rely on you to resolve all their conflicts for them.

Don't try to play detective. If you must step in, don't try to establish blame. This will only intensify the conflict and build resentment in the one who is blamed. Since it is unlikely in sibling conflict that either is truly blameless, it is better to hold both accountable when conflict and arguments arise. When sibling arguments start to spiral out of control, for example, use the occasion to dish out household chores. Not only will this separate the combatants, but you'll get some much needed help around the house.

Provide lots of compliments. The best intervention is prevention. One way to

Since it is unlikely in sibling conflict that either is truly blameless, it is better to hold both accountable when conflict and arguments arise.

prevent, or at least minimize, sibling rivalry is to give each child lots of attention for things that each does uniquely well. Just be careful that praise for one child is not received as criticism of the other. For example, do not say, "Gee, Christen, you really did a good job on your math homework. Caroline, how come you can't do as good a job on your math homework?" Especially be on the lookout for opportunities to praise sibling cooperation and effective conflict resolution.

Be an example of what you preach. If you and your spouse set a good example of ways of handling your own conflicts and arguments, your kids will be more likely to do so as well. Remember: The best sermon is a good example.

Don't automatically blame your teenager. Many parents view younger kids as "victims" in sibling conflict. While it is reasonable to expect more mature behavior from teenagers, it is important to keep in mind that younger siblings often have developed well-honed skills for irritating their older counterparts. So when you do discipline, discipline both.

Don't respond to tattling. Responding to tattling only begets more tattling. So, unless you actually enjoy hearing your kids whine and complain about each other, set a "no tattling" rule. With one exception: dangerous behavior. The prime directive in every household should be safety.

Allow for boundaries. Insist that siblings respect each other's personal belongings. Establish a household rule that no one should ever take anything that belongs to someone else without their permission. Everyone deserves to have

If handled correctly, sibling rivalry can turn what is frequently a difficult, frustrating, and painful experience into an opportunity for learning.

their personal property respected and to have a certain amount of personal "space." Even when siblings share a bedroom, make sure it is clear what is community property and space, and what is not.

Take heart. Sibling rivalry has always been with us, and always will. But that doesn't mean that parents cannot manage it effectively. In fact, if handled correctly, sibling rivalry can turn what is frequently a difficult, frustrating, and painful experience into an opportunity for learning effective conflict resolution skills and the value of cooperation over raw competition.

Despite the countless and often heated conflict that many adults had with their own siblings when growing up, today they usually count among their closest friends the siblings with which they fought the most when they were kids. Have confidence that someday, the same can be true of those screaming kids in your own household.

Sleep

"Bradley! Are you out of bed yet?"

"You're going to miss the school bus. Again!"

"BRAD-Leeeeeey!"

That's the way masses of parents begin the day—by trying to pry their young teens out of bed.

Are these kids just lazy slug-a-beds? Or are they just desperately tired?

Sleep researchers across the country say our teenagers are, in fact, desperately tired. And they believe they have isolated the reason for this exhaustion. No, don't blame the kids for going to bed too late. Instead, blame puberty.

Researchers have found that, as adolescents go through puberty, they need

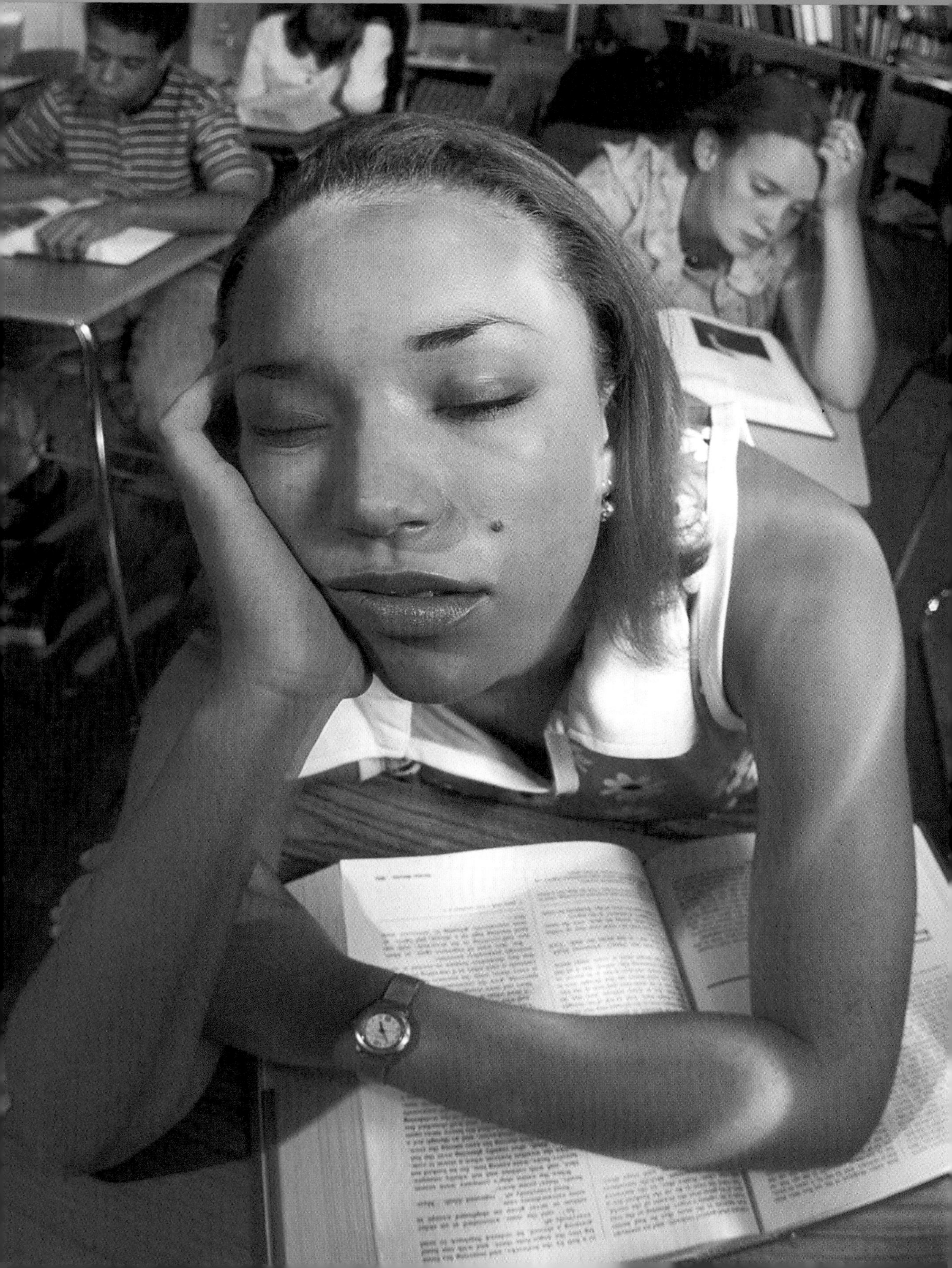

more sleep than ever. They should, in fact, be sleeping nine or nine and a half hours a night. (Most high school kids get between six and seven hours a night.)

"We have these kids so sleep-deprived, it's almost as if they are drugged," says James B. Maas, M.D., a sleep researcher at Cornell University in Ithaca, New York.

Kids Become Night People

Mary Carskadon, M.D., professor of psychiatry and human behavior at Brown University in Providence, Rhode Island, spearheaded the research that connected puberty and sleep deprivation in a 1991 study. She and her colleagues examined teen sleep patterns and found that when adolescents are going through puberty their biological clocks undergo a hormonal "phase shift" as they mature.

With this shift, the brain delays its release of the hormone melatonin, which helps to set the body's wake/sleep cycle (the circadian rhythm). The pineal gland in the

Twenty percent of our high school students fall asleep in school, and fully half of them claim they are not really alert until after 3 p.m.

brain releases melatonin at about 10:30 at night instead of 9:30. That, in turn, delays the desire to sleep. And it also delays the desire to wake up in the morning.

Dr. Carskadon, who is considered the preeminent researcher in the field of adolescent sleep, says that the reason it's so hard to get kids up early in the morning is because their natural circadian rhythm tells them they should be sleeping.

"These kids may be being asked to function at the wrong time for their bodies," she says.

So our teens wander like zombies through their first school periods. In fact, studies at the University of Minnesota show that 20 percent of our high school students fall asleep in school, and fully half of them claim they are not really alert until after 3 p.m.

Dr. Carskadon determined that early school start times may result in "grogginess, lack of attention in class, poor performance on exams, and increased odds of behavioral or disciplinary problems."

What's worse, if they are old enough to drive, sleep-deprived youngsters are vulnerable to catastrophic accidents, says Mark Hahowald, M.D., director of the Minnesota Regional Sleep Disorders Center at Hennepin County Medical Center in Minneapolis. And, he says, they also are more vulnerable to drugs and alcohol.

Dr. Carskadon began her research by studying sixth graders in 36 schools. She and her colleagues targeted sixth graders because they wanted students who would be close in age and social development but would also span several stages of puberty.

The students responded to questionnaires that queried them

Good Sleep Strategies

To help your teen get more sleep on school nights:

Do:

- Eliminate coffee, cola, and other caffeinated drinks after noon.
- Establish a soothing bedtime routine—for instance, taking a bath or listening to soft music.
- Encourage a regular bedtime hour.

Do Not:

- Suggest your teen give up an after-school activity to "save energy.'"
- Send your teen to bed early. (He or she will just stare at the ceiling until the melatonin kicks in.)

about their bedtimes, as well as what time of day they have the energy to participate in their favorite activities.

The researchers found that among the sixth graders, puberty had a significant influence on the pattern of sleeping late and rising late. Other factors—such as academic or social demands—had less of an effect.

Dr. Carskadon's research was a significant departure from the previously held belief that as children grew older they needed less sleep.

Resetting the School Bell

Dr. Carskadon's research prompted a 1994 letter from the Minnesota Medical Association to all school superintendents in the state, urging districts to eliminate

Researchers are tracking the data from these late-start schools and comparing it with early-start schools. Their preliminary findings suggest that students at schools with later starting times get better grades.

early starting hours in deference to teenagers' biological need to sleep longer.

And so today school districts in Minnesota, Oregon, and Virginia have changed the time they ring the first period bell. In Minnesota, instead of expecting middle school students to arrive at 7:15, they now come in at 9:40. High school begins at 8:40 instead of 7:15.

And the result? Teachers at Edina High School in Edina, Minnesota, generally agreed that during the first hour they "didn't have people with their heads down on the desk."

"The students seem to be more engaged in what they're doing; they seem to be more focused," the teachers reported.

Researchers are tracking the data from these late-start schools and comparing it with what they know about early-start schools. Their preliminary findings suggest that students at schools with later starting times get better grades.

Of course, if your teen doesn't go to a "late start" school, you still have the challenge of those early morning hours to contend with. (See "Good Sleep Strategies" on page 139 for coping techniques.)

Tobacco Scoreboard

Here's the score on what tobacco can do to your teenager in the future.

Smokers

- Heart attack
- Stroke
- Emphysema
- Cancer

Chewers

- Mouth cancer
- Pharynx cancer
- Larynx cancer
- Esophagus cancer
- Loss of teeth

Source: National Institute of Drug Abuse, National Institutes of Health.

Smoking

Your teenager came home reeking of tobacco. Then, a crumpled pack of butts fell out of a pair of jeans and right into the washing machine. Even though this is a moment you have dreaded, try not to lose your cool.

Hopefully, you have done some groundwork by having said in the past—long and loud—that you disapprove of smoking because it

why smoking is addictive

t he time comes in almost every smoker's life when he or she decides to quit. Teenaged smokers often come in for a big surprise when they discover that putting tobacco behind them is not as easy as they thought it was going to be. The coach says, "Quit." And guess what? They can't ... at least not without a struggle. The reason people continue to smoke even after they have learned that it might kill them is that they are addicted to nicotine.

When a person smokes tobacco, his or her lungs absorb nicotine. From there, the nicotine quickly moves into the bloodstream, where it is circulated throughout the brain. And nicotine hits the brain fast—in only about eight seconds.

For those who chew, nicotine enters the bloodstream through the mucous membranes that line the mouth.

Nicotine affects the entire body. It acts directly on the heart to change heart rate and blood pressure. It acts on the nerves that control respiration to change breathing patterns.

But nicotine's most important effect is in the brain, where it can stimulate feelings of pleasure.

Nicotine activates areas of the brain that produce feelings of pleasure and reward.

The brain has billions of nerve cells that communicate by releasing chemical messengers called neurotransmitters. Each neurotransmitter is like a key that fits into its own special lock, called a receptor. When a neurotransmitter finds its receptor, it activates the receptor's nerve cell.

Here's where nicotine gets tricky. Its molecule is shaped just like the neurotransmitter called acetylcholine. Acetylcholine is involved in many body functions, but here let's concentrate on the fact that it causes the release of other neurotransmitters and hormones that affect mood, appetite, memory, and more. When nicotine gets into the brain, it attaches to acetylcholine receptors and mimics the actions of acetylcholine.

Nicotine also activates areas of the brain that produce feelings of pleasure and reward.

So I smoked a couple cigarettes with some friends. It's not a big deal. I've never bought a pack of cigarettes, and I don't plan on it. It's just a social thing I've done a few times. I'm NOT addicted to cigarettes.

Then stop now before you are addicted! Nicotine plays games with the chemicals in your brain, and it doesn't take much to become addicted. Once you are addicted to cigarettes, it's extrememly difficult to quit.

Recently, scientists discovered that nicotine raises the levels of a neurotransmitter called dopamine—which is sometimes called the pleasure molecule. Dopamine is the very same neurotransmitter that is involved in addictions to other drugs, such as cocaine and heroin.

Researchers now believe that this change in dopamine may play a key role in all addictions. Perhaps tobacco's connection with dopamine explains why some people find it so darned hard to stop smoking.

can ruin a person's health. You will have to trust that the antismoking seed you've planted is still buried somewhere in you adolescent's nicotine-addled brain.

Smoking Stinks

Now it's time to sit down and have a serious talk. But don't start out talking about emphysema and lung cancer. Your teenager—like every other teenager on the planet—is Invincible, Invulnerable, and Immortal. Those kinds of things happen to oooold people—not to the hip and cool.

Instead, talk about how smoking gives people smelly breath, smelly clothes, and stinky hair. Calculate how much money will be spent in a week, in a month, and in a year on cigarettes.

Smoking Across America

A group called the Campaign for Tobacco Free Kids has studied the smoking habits of teens across the nation. Here's some of what they found.

- In Alaska—36.5 percent of high school kids smoke cigarettes and 23.5 percent chew tobacco.

- In Colorado, smoking is pervasive, with 33.7 percent smoking.

- In Kentucky, a tobacco state, the number is 34.1 percent smoking, and an astonishing 39 percent chewing tobacco.

- In Delaware, the number who smoke is up to 34.5 percent.

- In Indiana, 37.8 percent of high school kids smoke.

- In Missouri, 39.8 percent of 12th-graders are smoking cigarettes.

- But West Virginia has the dubious distinction of having the smoking-est students, with 43.3 percent lighting up, and 34.5 percent chewing tobacco!

However, there are some bright spots:

- In health-conscious California, only 22.2 percent of the high school students smoke, and only about 7.3 percent of the boys chew tobacco.

- Washington, D.C., has similar numbers, with 22 percent smoking and 2.3 percent of the boys chewing.

Also talk about the social stigma attached to smoking. Tell your son or daughter about your coworkers who have to stand out in the rain to get their mid-morning nicotine fix—and how others snicker at them.

Next, gather together some magazine ads for cigarettes that are obviously aimed at the next generation of nicotine addicts. Point out to your teen that he or she is being manipulated—used!—by big business and advertising. That tactic usually puts them in high dudgeon!

The Start of Stopping

Usually a kid doesn't start smoking alone. He'll be riding in a car with friends when someone lights up and passes the pack around. Everyone else is smoking, and no teenager wants to feel like some nerdy jerk, so he lights up. Or she'll be with her friends at the mall, gathered at a table in the food court. Her girlfriends will say that, even though they're hungry, they prefer not to eat. The food is too fattening. Instead, they take out their cigarettes and puff away. Naturally, she joins them.

Plot how to say no. One important step in quitting is finding a way for your teenager to remain friends with smokers without actually being a smoker. Discuss this topic with your teen, so that you can come up with an acceptable way to decline the offer of a cigarette or a cigarette break.

Find better things to do. Also encourage your teen to become involved in the school band, a sports team, or any group activity at all where smoking is discouraged.

Set that all important example. If you or your spouse smoke cigarettes, your situation is more difficult. You can handle it one of two ways: Declare your house a smoke-free zone and do your smoking away from home, or you and your teen can give up smoking together.

Fight the urge. Remind your teen that the urge to light up lasts less than a minute—so suggest that he or she ride out the urge and eliminate at least that one cigarette.

Seek help. If all your efforts fail, haul your teenager to the family doctor. The doctor is well trained in counseling teens about tobacco and may be able to suggest specific ways to get off the weed.

Sports Injuries

"Injury remains the most underrecognized major public health problem in this country," says David H. Janda, M.D., director of the Institute for Preventative Sports Medicine in Ann Arbor, Michigan.

And the simplest, yet most effective, way to prevent sports injuries is to teach the fundamentals of the sport, he says.

"We at the institute can't overemphasize the importance of instructing players on the proper techniques of their sport, such as sliding in baseball or heading the ball in soccer, so they can play safely," Dr. Janda says.

"For example, some children playing in leagues using the softer, heavier baseballs are not instructed on how to get out of the way of a pitch coming right at them. Many of these children are also assured by their coaches that because the baseball is softer, the risk for injury is much less."

Tests at the institute, however, showed that the balls were no better than traditional balls, "and in some cases made the injuries worse," says Dr. Janda.

Dangerous Games

The most dangerous games are football for boys and gymnastics for girls. Football players suffer knee and ankle injuries, but head and neck injuries are not uncommon. In gymnastics, leg injuries—especially the knees and ankles—are

Why Teens Smoke

Seattle teens responded to a survey that asked them which different feelings or situations trigger the need to smoke. Here are their answers:

- Anger and arguments
- School pressures
- Troubles at home
- Wanting to appear glamorous or grown-up
- Loneliness
- Feeling uptight
- Breaking up
- Boredom
- Parties
- Rewarding yourself
- Feeling of rebellion
- Friends or family smoking
- After eating or drinking alcohol
- Hunger

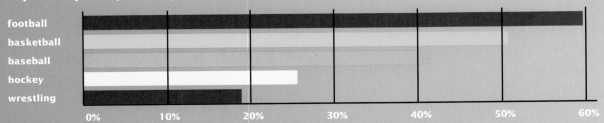

Top five sports youth ages 13 to 17 regularly listen to or watch:

football
basketball
baseball
hockey
wrestling

0%   10%   20%   30%   40%   50%   60%

Source: "The Mood of American Youth," The Horatio Alger Association of Distinguished Americans, Inc., Alexandria, VA., 1996.

most common. However, some gymnasts have suffered serious back injuries.

But even playing one of the safer sports can lead to injuries. Baseball and softball players are prone to foot and ankle injuries from sliding into base. Basketball players suffer leg injuries.

Bicycling, a very popular recreational sport, can be hazardous for kids who do not wear bike helmets. Some 300 children are killed each year, and an astonishing 400,000 visit emergency rooms. The biggest dangers are cars and poor road conditions that cause a kid to be thrown off the bike.

Boxers are prone to both brain and eye injuries. Soccer players get hurt when they slam into goalposts or get kicked in the leg by another player. They also may develop headaches—even mild concussions, says Dr. Janda—from heading the ball.

Preventing Injury: A Checklist for Team Sports

When your son or daughter signs up for a team, in some sense you also sign up for that team. It's in your teen's best interest for you to attend games and meetings to see how things are run.

Each year millions of preadolescent children and teenagers participate in organized athletics. Doctors at the American Academy of Pediatrics are concerned because coaches in community-based programs often have no formal training in coaching. And, they say, the credentials and training of school coaches are highly variable.

The American Academy of Pediatrics recommends that every sports program should provide adequate safeguards by requiring:

- A preparticipation physical examination at least every two years
- Warm-up procedures
- Availability of a medically trained person who can recognize significant injuries during practices and games of contact sports
- Policies for first-aid, referral of injured participants, treatment, rehabilitation, and certification for return to participation
- Suitable and well-maintained sports facilities
- Appropriate protective equipment
- Strict enforcement of rules concerning safety
- A formal surveillance method to ensure that goals are met

You'll be doing all the students at your adolescent's school a big favor if you and other parents insist that these criteria be met.

The Psychology of Teen Sports

More than 20 million American children participate in organized sports, some starting as young as 4 years of age. In addition to providing physical exercise and helping teens master fundamental

How to Treat a Sprain

When your young athlete twists an ankle or overstretches a joint, the damage that results to the ligaments inside the joint is called a sprain. Kids usually sprain their ankles, knees, or the arches of their feet.

If your teen is complaining of pain, but the joint is not swollen or bruised, you can suspect a slight sprain. A moderate sprain will be a bit swollen and black-and-blue. Your teen will find it difficult and painful to move the joint. In a severe sprain, you teen's joint will be swollen and black-and-blue, and he or she will not be able to put any weight on it.

Call your doctor if the pain is moderate or severe. An X ray may be necessary to determine whether a bone has been broken.

In all cases, wrap the joint with an elastic bandage to protect it and prevent further injury. And apply ice to reduce swelling and pain. Elevate the injured joint, especially overnight, so that it's above the level of the heart. Rest the joint by avoiding all activities that cause pain.

skills, under the best of circumstances sports also teach important lessons, such as focusing on the team, rather than the self; learning good sportsmanship and effective conflict resolution skills; and learning how to set goals and work toward achieving them.

Unfortunately, participation in sports does not always occur under the best of circumstances. Rather than providing fun and physical exercise, too often sports

When coaches and parents put too much pressure on teens to win, they foster the development of aggression, rather than healthy competition.

become another source of stress for kids. One study found that 73 percent drop out of sports programs by age 13. The number one reason? Sports burnout.

Even worse, when adult coaches and parents put too much pressure on teens to win, participation in sports can foster the development of aggression, rather than healthy competition. And for the second stringers, sports may only create a sense of inadequacy, rather than competency.

Here are some tips to help ensure that your teen's participation in sports is a healthy and positive experience:

Be on your own best behavior. When at your teen's sporting events, set an example of good sportsmanship yourself.

Stress playing fair over winning. Encourage your teen to play hard, but always

safe skating

n-line skating is a young sport on the rise. The American Academy of Pediatrics reports that about 18 million kids under 18-years-old are skating.

The Academy says it's a great sport because it provides a good aerobic workout and allows kids a means of independent transportation.

Doctors, however, stress that protective gear is an absolute necessity for anyone who does in-line skating. They strongly advise fitting kids out with a helmet, wrist guards, knee pads, and elbow pads.

Wrist guards are an especially good idea because they can prevent broken wrists, the most common in-line skating injury.

The greatest dangers for in-line skaters are cars and road hazards. So, to get your teenager off to a good start, begin skating at an indoor roller rink. Once the young skater has mastered the basics, move on to a paved hike/bike trail where there are no motor vehicles.

The skates you select are important, too. Beginners should start with three- or four-wheel skates. Five-wheel skates are only for the superstars. As the skates are used, check that the brake pads are not worn down and that the wheels are worn evenly and turn freely.

Also strongly warn your teenager about the dangers of "skitching," a dangerous technique in which the skater grabs a moving car or truck and holds on. If the vehicle stops or turns suddenly, the skater will be thrown loose while traveling very fast. Impact with the road or with another car can end in very serious injury.

within the rules. Winning is important, but it's not the most important thing. Never, never encourage your teen to cheat or bend the rules in order to win.

Encourage individual skill development. Rather than comparing your teen to other players, focus on helping your teen set reasonable, measurable, and achievable objectives with the goal of helping your teen achieve his or her individual potential.

Don't overemphasize sports. While participation in sports ought to be encouraged, make sure you praise your child at least as much for what they do in the classroom as for what they do on the athletic field.

Teasing and Bullying

If your teenager complains that he or she is being teased or bullied, listen up! Bullying is a serious problem among children and teenagers, says Dan Olweus, Ph.D., one of the world's leading experts on the problem.

Most kids either do not tell adults that they are being bullied, or they wait a very long time to share the problem. (Kids worry about retaliation—that "telling" will just make matters worse.) So, if your teenager has come to you with this issue, step in immediately.

Bullying isn't just silly kid stuff. Youngsters who are bullied experience significant psychological harm, which can interfere with their social, academic, and emotional development, says Dr. Olweus, a Swedish researcher who teaches at the University of Bergen in Norway.

Bullying is any kind of ongoing physical or verbal mistreatment of a child by another child or a group of children. The hallmark of bullying is an imbalance of power: A big kid picking on a smaller, weaker one; or a group of kids ganging up on an individual.

Parents and teachers are often unaware of just how much bullying really goes on—because it happens in places that are not well supervised. The arenas for bullies include school hallways, the streets leading to and from school, the school bus, and the playground or playing fields.

Studies in several countries have shown that at least 15 percent of students in schools are involved—9 percent are victims, while another 6 or 7 percent bully others repeatedly.

Bullying can take many forms, such as physical violence and attacks, verbal taunts, name-calling and put-downs, threats and intimidation, extortion or stealing money and possessions, or a more subtle exclusion from the peer group.

What Makes a Bully

In several studies, bullies have been shown to be physically stronger than the average kid. Most often, bullies are boys—but girls can be bullies, too. Generally, bullies are not happy people. They don't like school, and they often have problems at home. Bullies tend to report a lack of attention and warmth from their parents. In addition, one parent may bully the other—providing a strong negative role model as the bully grows into adolescence.

Dr. Olweus's research has shown that bullies are highly aggressive and may have what he calls a general conduct disorder. He says it is a myth that bullies are insecure underneath their swagger. Rather, their self-esteem is usually average or even above average.

His follow-up research also shows that when bullies grow up they are three to four times more likely than normal youngsters to be convicted of crimes.

What Makes a Victim

Teenagers who are attacked usually are small, quiet, and physically weak. They tend to have a low sense of self-worth and a high level of depression. Often their classmates—and their teachers, too—see them as somehow differing from the norm.

Parents of these kids are often described as overprotective.

These kids usually don't know how to handle themselves in a confrontation. Not only don't they fight back, they often don't even defend themselves. As a result, they become easy marks.

To compound the matter, these kids are not good at making friends. So when they are attacked by a bully, they usually have to face the bully alone.

There is another type of victim, as well. Not timid or shy, members of this subgroup act in impulsive, inappropriate, and irritating ways. These so-called "provocative victims" also may try to bully others—so they are both bullies and victims.

Ways You Can Help

Watch for signs of bullying. Not all teens tell their parents that they are being victimized, so be on the lookout for the following:
• Withdrawal
• Sudden loss of interest in school
• Fear of going to school
• A drop in grades
• Signs of physical abuse, torn clothing, missing money, missing possessions

Don't go it alone. If your teenager is being bullied at school, tell the school's principal at once. Put together a written report for the school principal that includes:
• The names of the bullies

Quick Sketch of a Bully

Here are the most common traits among bullies:

- They want power.
- They are focused on their own pleasure.
- They will use others to get what they want.
- They appear to take satisfaction from inflicting injury on others.
- They have trouble seeing things from someone else's point of view.
- They have little empathy for their victims.

Quick Sketch of a Victim

These are some of the traits shared by victims:

- They are usually anxious, insecure, sensitive, and quiet.
- They have a low sense of self-worth.
- They usually don't fight back.
- They lack social skills.
- They tend to have fewer friends.
- They are often physically smaller than classmates.

- When the incidents occurred
- Where they occurred
- A basic description of what happened

Get the parties together. Ask for a school meeting with you, your teen, the principal, the bully, and the bully's parents to discuss the problem and find ways to resolve it. Be aware that one common trait of bullies is that they tend to minimize their wrongdoing.

Look at the bigger picture. Suggest that the school initiate a comprehensive antibullying program.

Practice prevention. Suggest that your teenager stay away from kids who act like bullies. And help your teen develop the ability to shrug off insults that bullies like to spew.

Counter a negative with a positive. Remind your teen to give himself or herself a silent pep talk whenever being picked on. ("They can call me a moron all they want. I know that I'm actually pretty intelligent. So who cares what they say!")

Seek out friends. Encourage your teen to join group activities. It's one way for a

what if the bully is your kid?

You receive a call from the school advising you that your son has been stalking one of his classmates, making anonymous threatening phone calls to his home, and scaring the daylights out of him. You are asked to attend a meeting with this boy and his parents. (This scenario can, and does, happen with girls, too. But it's far more likely to be a boy problem.)

Focus on positive change. You're angry and probably ashamed. Try to get past those feelings so that you can intercede effectively in the situation. Kids who bully others often have trouble in other relationships, too. If you can help your teenager change the pattern of his behavior toward others, you may be able to help him have a happier future.

Communicate. Begin by talking to your teen about his actions. Don't let him get away with saying that "it was no big deal." It is a big deal to abuse another person, even if it's just with words.

Do discipline your teen. State clearly that you will not tolerate bullying behavior. Arrange for an effective, nonviolent punishment that fits the circumstances.

Be there. Spend more time with your teen, and supervise his activities more closely. Set reasonable curfews.

Support change. Cooperate with the school in modifying your teen's aggressive behavior.

Be a cheerleader. Lavish him with praise over the efforts he makes toward responsible behavior and for following the rules at home and at school.

Eliminate violent role models. Monitor your family's television and entertainment choices. As a family, do not watch violent television shows (including cartoons), and get rid of violent computer games.

Watch for any overly aggressive or violent behavior in the family—and put a stop to it.

Seek professional help. Ask for help from the school psychologist or a social worker in working out your teen's problem behaviors.

shy teenager to make friends. And a teen with a couple of buddies nearby is much less vulnerable to abuse.

Encourage assertive responses. Teach your teen to be assertive when confronted by a bully. It's appropriate to say, "Leave me alone," or "Don't bother me." But your teen should try to give just one assertive response, or the bullying may escalate.

Stress the importance of body language. Share with your teen the following tricks to get the bully to back off:

- First, take a few deep breaths to help stay calm.
- Hold yourself confidently.
- Keep your hands steady.
- Don't look down at the ground or at your feet.
- Maintain eye contact.

Know when to get help. In a dangerous confrontation, advise your teen to walk away and to find an adult who will help.

Teasing: When to Laugh It Off

There isn't a person alive who hasn't been teased—sometimes unmercifully—by friend and foe alike. And there are days when your teen will be teased, too.

Teasing can be embarrassing—even humiliating—but it's usually not malicious. In fact, if the teaser sees that the teasing is really upsetting someone, he or she will usually back off. And maybe even apologize.

"Hey, 'Brenda-Braces.' I hear you broke the metal detector at the airport."

"Your mother dresses you funny!"

"Here comes little Miss Perfect. All As all the time. Teacher's pet."

"Some kids learn how to drive. And then there's you!"

"Hey pizza-face. Pop any good zits lately? What? Did they run out of zit gunk at the drugstore?"

Sometimes a remark can hurt when it strikes close to home. But most teasing is not meant to really hurt. It's meant (mostly) to make the teaser look smart and the kid being teased look dumb.

Teasing can be embarrassing—even humiliating—but it's usually not malicious. In fact, if the teaser sees that the teasing is really upsetting someone, he or she will usually back off. And maybe even apologize.

If your teenager has been hurt by teasing, listen to the story with a kind ear. But advise your son or daughter to try to laugh it off. If teasing is coming from a friend, and it's starting to get to your teen, suggest that they have a little heart-to-heart talk. If the teasing is just snide remarks made by random schoolmates, advise your teen to ignore it.

Television

t he average American teenager spends 1,500 hours each year sitting in front of a television set. In comparison, that same American teenager spends only 900 hours sitting in a classroom.

Studies show that excessive TV watching is associated with all sorts of bad things, such as poor school performance, a diminished attention span, and an increase in aggressive behavior. Too much television watching also makes teens feel less secure and worry more that they will be a victim of crime. Teens who watch a lot of TV also evidence lower social trust and are less engaged with peers.

And if all that isn't enough, TV also makes kids fat. According to the federal government's Third National Health and Nutrition Examination Survey, 8- to 16-year-olds who watched four or more hours of TV a day were, on average, 17 percent heavier than those who watched less than two hours of TV a day. That's because kids who watch TV a lot are less likely to engage in physical exercise. Indeed, one study found that whereas only 37 percent of students in grades 9 through 12 engage in physical exercise at least three times per week, more than 90 percent watch TV every day.

The negative effects of kids watching too much TV is not confined to childhood. In a 20-year study of more than 300 Chicago-area children, L. Rowell Huesmann, Ph.D., of the University of Michigan's Institute for Social Research found the more violent television a child watched at ages 6 through 8, the more aggressive behavior that child displayed 15 years later upon becoming an adult. For example, 16.7 percent of the young adult women who had watched a lot of television violence as girls reported having punched, beaten, or choked another adult, compared to only 3.6 percent of young adult women who had not watched a lot of television violence as kids.

For young adult men, the rates were even higher. Thirty-seven percent of the

TV Facts

98	Percent of American households that own a TV
2.5	The number of TV sets in the average U.S. Household
3.75	The number of hours the average American watches TV each day
66	Percent of Americans who regularly watch TV while eating dinner
38	Number of minutes per week the average parent spends in meaningful conversation with their children
1,680	Number of minutes per week the average child spends watching TV
52	Percent of children ages 5 to 17 who have a TV in their bedroom
54%	Percent of 4- to 6-year-olds who would rather watch television than spend time with their fathers
20,000	Number of commercials the average teen sees each year
200,000	Number of acts of violence the average child will see on TV by the time he or she turns 18

Source: TV-Free America, 1611 Connecticut Ave., NW, Suite 3A, Washington, DC 20009

young men who had watched a good deal of television violence as children reported having thrown something at a partner during an argument, compared to only 16 percent of low-violence television viewers.

In addition to the violence, television also displays casual and frequent sex as the norm, coarse and lewd language as acceptable, kids being disrespectful to parents and other adults as being without consequence, and religion as silly, anachronistic, or destructive. In 1961, Newton Minow, then chairman of the Federal Communications Commission, described television as "a vast wasteland" of violence, formulas, commercials, and boredom. It's only gotten worse since then.

But it's not just the content of television shows that is the problem. Research suggests that the passive nature of TV watching may lead to diminished nerve development and brain growth in children. So even if your teen is watching 4 hours of news, documentaries, and public television a day, that is still too much TV.

Tune Out Too Much TV

What's the answer?

Turn off the TV. If you can't turn it off completely, severely limit the amount of time your teen can watch.

Set time limits. Restrict TV viewing to the weekends only. That way, TV won't interfere with more important things, like homework. And on weekends, your teen will be more interested in hanging out with friends than hanging out at home watching TV.

Put schoolwork first. At the very least, insist on a "no TV" rule until after all homework is completed.

Enjoy silence. Never allow the use of TV as background noise. The TV should be turned on only for certain shows and turned off immediately after the show is over.

Go for quality. The TV you do allow your teens to watch should be television that teaches and reinforces the values you want them to learn. That means watching more of such things as American Movie Classics, The Discovery Channel, and The Learning Channel, and fewer network sitcoms, music videos, and made-for-cable TV movies.

Be informed. One good place you can go for information on the content of

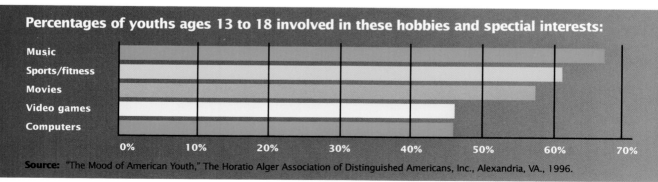

Percentages of youths ages 13 to 18 involved in these hobbies and special interests:

Music
Sports/fitness
Movies
Video games
Computers

0% 10% 20% 30% 40% 50% 60% 70%

Source: "The Mood of American Youth," The Horatio Alger Association of Distinguished Americans, Inc., Alexandria, VA., 1996.

television shows is the website (www.parentstv.org) of the Parents' Television Council, which provides ratings of network shows according to content.

Be prepared for a fight. When you first restrict your teen's television time, expect a few arguments. Some are so used to endless hours of staring at a television screen, they will go through a sort of withdrawal when their TV viewing is restricted. But don't back down. Eventually, your teen will discover there is more

Research has found that the more violent television a child watched at ages 6 through 8, the more aggressive behavior that child displayed 15 years later upon becoming an adult.

to life than television. As a first step, you might want to participate in the National TV-Turnoff Week, held in April each year.

Set a good example. Now, here's the really bad news. Limiting TV watching for your teen means limiting TV watching for yourself as well. It's not going to work if you say to your teen, "No TV except on weekends," and then you watch three or four hours of TV yourself every evening.

Do something else. Trade off TV viewing for time spent doing other activities, like reading. One psychologist suggests permitting a teen to watch one minute of TV for every minute spent reading.

What else, you may ask, can you and your teen do instead? Here are just a few ideas:

- Read
- Learn to dance
- Write a letter
- Ride a bike
- Go fishing
- Volunteer in your community
- Go for a walk
- Have a conversation
- Go to the library
- Cook
- Watch a sunset
- Plant a garden
- Play a board game together
- Listen to music
- Fix something around the house
- Exercise

You get the idea. There really is more to life than TV. Unplug the beast, and discover what you've both been missing.

index

i

Identity, personal, 33–34

Independence
allowing for, 56–57
and money, 57–58

Infectious mononucleosis, 127–129

Influences on teens
community activities, 54
parents, 10, 49–50
peers, 42–43
religion, 54, 90, 110
television, 46
Inhalants, 94

Injuries, sports
dangerous games, 143–144
prevention of, 145
and psychology of teen
sports, 145–147

Inoculation scheduling, 21

Internet
e-mail, 74
dangers, 38–39

Iron, 29, 31
Iron-deficiency anemia, 29–30

j

Jobs, 113–118
goals of, 117–118
parental agreement on, 115–116
teen worker's bill of rights, 116

k

Kissing disease, 127–129

l

Lacto-ovo vegetarians, 31
Lactose intolerance, 30
Learning disabilities, 88–89

Love
discipline as part of, 51–52
for effective parenting, 51–52
for non-communicative
teens, 35–36

Low self-esteem
non-competitive activities for, 127
parenting styles linked to, 125–126
as risk factor in reckless
behavior, 41
signs of, 126–127

LSD, 93
Luteinizing hormone-releasing
hormone (LHRH), 16

m

Magazines, 118
Male puberty, 16–18
Marijuana, 93
Marital happiness, tips for, 68–69

Marital problems of parents
couples mentoring for, 71
and effect on teens, 65–66
tips for teen-proofing, 68–70

Marriage Encounter, 70
MDMA hallucinogenic, 93
Meat, 27–29
Melatonin, 139
Menarche, 20

Menstruation
iron deficiency caused by, 29–30
talks about, 14–15, 20–21

Mescaline, 93
Methamphetamine, 93
Methaqualone, 93
Migraine headaches, 123–124
Milk, 30
Mites, dust, 95–96

Money
allowances, 57–58
as employment goal, 117
spending habits of teens, 117

Monitoring, parental
and high-risk behavior, 40–41
of Internet use, 38–39
of sexual behavior, 107
tips, 45

Mononucleosis, 127–129

Moodiness
from PMS, 133–135
reasons for, 10

Mothers, parenting style of, 67

Motor vehicle accidents
alcohol-related, 38, 90
from reckless driving, 37–38

n

Nicotine addiction, 141

Nutrition
breakfast, 25, 28
calorie needs, 24, 26
dairy food, 30
fat, 30
fiber, 29
grains, 27–28
importance of, 23–24
meat, 27–29
for vegetarians, 31

Nutrition labels
fat content on, 30
reading, 26–27

o

Oral contraceptives
for acne, 86
limitations of, 108

Overweight teens
exercise for, 132–133
low-cal snacks for, 131
medical help for, 130

p

Parental consent survey, 53

Parental monitoring
and high-risk behavior, 40–41
of Internet use, 38–39
of sexual behavior, 107

Parenting, effective
consistency for, 54–55
limit-setting for, 52–54

Parenting styles
of fathers, 66–67
self-esteem linked to, 125–126

Parents
divorcing or divorced, 71–78
marital happiness of, 65–71
moms versus dads, 67–68
stepparents, 78–81

Paxil, 110
PCP, 93

Peers
fear of rejection by, 44–45
importance of, 42–43
monitoring, 45

Personality
easygoing, 47, 61
types, 61

Pets
dander from, 96
death of, 121

Piercing, body, 99–100
Popularity, 42–43
Precocious puberty, 17

Pregnancy
precautions against, 107–108
as result of risk-taking behavior, 37
statistics, 102

Premenstrual syndrome
(PMS), 133–135

**Problem behavior and attention deficit
hyperactivity disorder, 88**
behavioral contracting for,
59–60, 62–63, 88
responses to, 62–63

Progesterone, 84
Prozac, 110, 124

Meet the Authors

Wade F. Horn

Wade F. Horn, Ph.D., is a clinical child psychologist and president of the National Fatherhood Initiative. He is also the former U.S. Commissioner for Children, Youth and Families, and former Chief of the U.S. Children's Bureau. He is the co-author of several books, including the *Better Homes and Gardens® New Father Book.* He lives in Gaithersburg, Maryland, with his wife and two teenage daughters.

Acknowledgments

I am indebted to Risa Garon, LCSW, of Children of Separation and Divorce Center, for sharing her expertise on ways to communicate effectively with teens about impending divorce, and to Steve Watters, M.A., and Candice Watters, M.A., both of Focus on the Family, for their insights on parental monitoring of the Internet. I am also deeply indebted to my wife Claudia and Christen Horn and Laura Aizkalns for reviewing the manuscript. Finally, I'd like to thank photographer Chip Simons for his unique photographs, Ken Carlson for his extraordinary book design, and Alice Feinstein whose editorial skills and vision made it all possible.

Carol Keough

Carol Keough survived the passage through the adolescence of her two sons Bradley and Jeffrey. She claims it is no coincidence that her first gray hair appeared on the same day her oldest boy got his driver's license. Her other books include the *Better Homes and Gardens® New Baby Book, Natural Relief for Arthritis,* and *Water Fit to Drink.* She lives in Chalfont, Pennsylvania, with her husband.

Acknowledgments

I sincerely thank my wonderful editor and friend Alice Feinstein for her support, guidance, and fine editing. I also would like to thank those in the medical community who were kind enough to share their valuable time with me. Special thanks to Henry J. Gault, M.D.; Mark Hahowald, M.D.; Anita Hirsch, R.D.; David H. Janda, M.D.; Sloan Beth Karver, M.D.; and Mitch Spero, Psy. D.